DRAUGHTSMAN MECHANICAL MCQ

OBJECTIVE QUESTION ANSWERS

MANOJ DOLE

Digitization is the need of the time. In the future, training in industrial training institutes will need to be conducted using online internet to make training more convenient and easy. E-books containing a set of MCQ questions will be made available to the trainees as they need to be more accustomed to the multiple choice questions MCQ to prepare for the online exams taking place in their industrial training institutes.

With all these factors in mind, Mr. Manoj Madhukar Dole Instructor, Industrial Training Institute, Satara, has written books according to the new annual system and NSQF-5 syllabus. And they've created theoretical mobile apps and blogs to make training easier, and made all these educational materials available for download on the world famous websites Google Play Store, Amazon and Apple Book Store.

The books were published by Hon'ble Joint Director Shri Rajendra Ghume Saheb Regional Office of Vocational Education and Training, Pune on 9/1/2019, at this time Shri Prakash Saigavkar Saheb Principal Government Industrial Training Institute Aundh Pune, Shri Tukaram Misal Saheb Principal Govt. Q. Sanstha Satara, Shri Sachin Dhumal Saheb District Vocational Education and Training Officer Satara, Shri Yatin Pargaonkar Saheb Principal Govt. Q. Sanstha Kolhapur, Shri Vikas Teke Saheb Inspector Vocational Education and Training Regional Office Pune, Palekar Foods Products Pvt. Ltd. Entrepreneurial Chairman of Satara Mr. Nilkanthrao Palekar Saheb, Chairman of Hira Foods Mr. Ibrahim Baba Tamboli Saheb, Mrs. Shalmali Pawar Headmaster Government Technical School Center Satara and other dignitaries were present on the occasion.

Contents

Foreword

Vocational education and training is imparted through the Department of Vocational Education and Training through the Department of Business Education and Business Practical to supply multi-skilled artisans in line with the rapidly growing demand in the industrial sector in the 21st century. All the occupations within the institutions are important, as the trainees from these occupations develop multi-skills as per the demands of the industry.

with the noble intention of making available MCQ e-books suitable for all businesses, considering that all the examinations in all the industries in the industrial sector are conducted online and include MCQ method questions. Mr. Manoj Madhukar Dole has written a very good e-book on MCQ method as per the new annual syllabus. This e-book will definitely be a guide for all the trainees, trainee candidates, training instructors and others concerned.

The author of the book is Mr. Manoj Madhukar Dole, Instructor Gov. ITI Satara has 17 years of training experience. Written as a new annual pattern, this e-book incorporates modern digital QR Code technology to understand the layout, simple language, and simple syntax, diagrams and videos for each subject. So I am sure that this e-book will definitely be useful for in-depth study and exam practice. The work they have done is certainly commendable.

Mr. Tukaram Misal
Principal Government Industrial Training Institute Satara.

Preface

DGET New Delhi and CSTARI Kolkata have been implementing an annual pattern for all businesses in ITI since the August 2018 session. The examination system will also be changed and it will be online from this year and since all the questions are of Objective Type (MCQ), the trainees are in dire need of in-depth study. It is with this in mind that we are delighted to present the books based on the old NIMI pattern and a complete overview of the new annual pattern, and we hope that these books will be a guide for all business directors and trainees. Is.

For writing these books, Johar Awate Saheb, Principal of ITI Akluj. Former Principal of ITI Satara Saigavkar Saheb, Assistant Director Shri Chandrakant Dhekne Saheb Regional Office of Vocational Education and Training, Pune, District Vocational Education and Training Officer Sachin Dhumal Saheb and Headmaster Government Technical School Kendra Shalmali Pawar Madam and son Adhiraj Dole, mother Kusum Dole, I am very grateful to my father Madhukar Dole and wife Ashwini Dole for their special guidance and cooperation from time to time.

Also, in a very short period of time, the book was reviewed by Shri Rajendra Ghume Saheb, Joint Director, Vocational Education and Training Regional Office, Pune, for his invaluable time in publishing the book. I am sincerely grateful for their feedback.

I am grateful to the Instructor of ITI Satara for there continuous support from the very beginning of writing the book.

From this book, I consider myself blessed to have shared my thoughts on e-learning with you. I will not claim that this book is perfect, because considering the perfection, this book is an attempt and is in its infancy. They will be valuable for improvement if they are tested and suggested.

Manoj Dole
Dated 9/1/2019

Acknowledgements

The industrial training and theoretical examination system of our industrial training institutes and these changes have been accepted by the craft instructors and the trainees. Theoretical examinations conducted in your industrial training institutes are also conducted online. Since these examinations are of multiple choice MCQ method, the trainees will need to get more practice of such questions.

With all these considerations in mind, Mr. Manoj Madhukar, Director, Dole Crafts, Katari Industrial Training Institute, Satara, has done a thorough study and with his diligent work and added his keen intellect, according to the new annual system and NSQF-5 syllabus, e-book of Katari and other machine trades. -Book) and they have created mobile apps and blogs on theoretical topics to make training easier and have made all these educational materials available for download on the world famous websites Google Play Store, Amazon and Apple Book Store. Training has been made easier by creating a print version and using advanced techniques like QR Code.

All these educational materials will definitely be a guide for all the trainees for in-depth study and for the craft instructors and other concerned who are imparting vocational training.

Draughtsman Mechanical MCQ Drawings

Online Test Exam
ITI Books
CNC Course
AutoCAD CAM
JOB & Apprentice
Online Theory
Computer Course
Trading Course
Web Designing
MSCIT Course
Shopping Business
Internet Business
Remotasks Course
Online Services
Top Sportsmans
Indian Army
Freedom Fighters
Top Scientists
Social Reformers
Motivational Speaker
Top Richest People
Join WhatsApp Group
Join Facebook Group
Like Facebook Page
PAN / Adhar / Licence
Passport

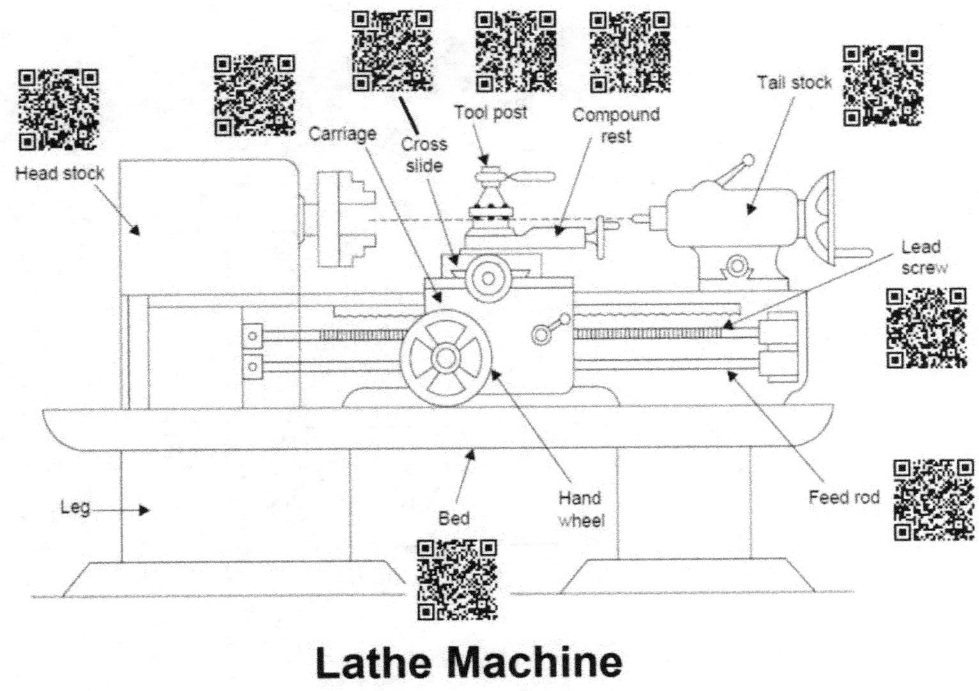

Lathe Machine

• 4 •

PLAIN OR HORIZONTAL MILLING MACHINE
Cutter
Arbor
Over arm
Table
Saddle
Column
Knee
Elevating screw
Base

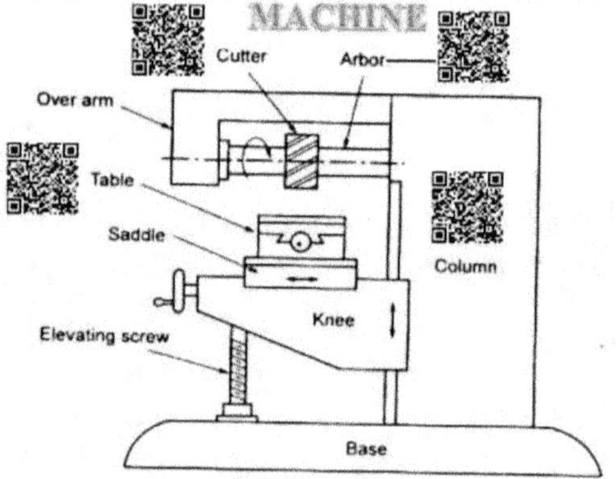

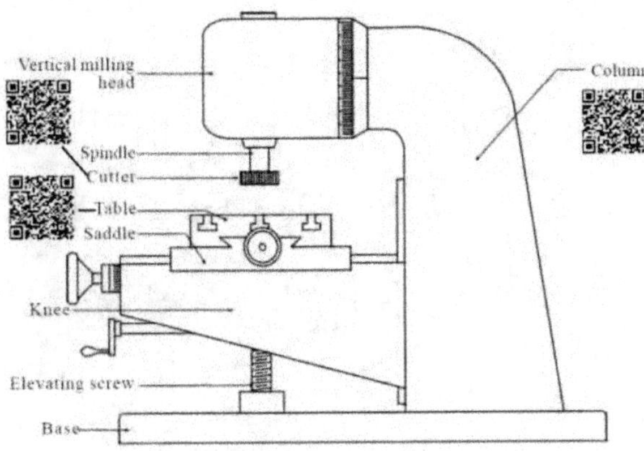

Vertical Milling Machine

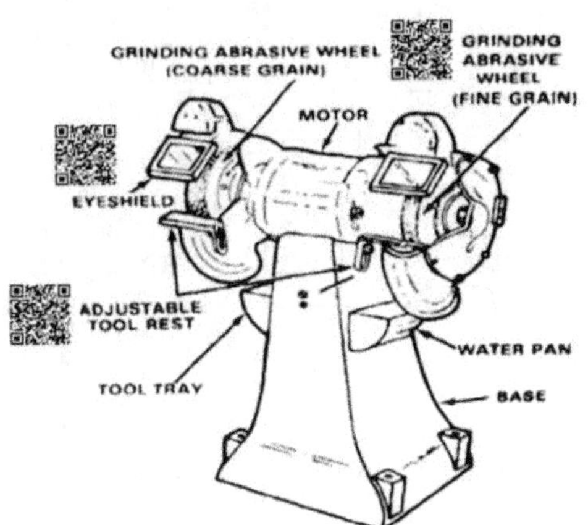

Pedastal Grinding Machine

DOUBLE HOUSING PLANER

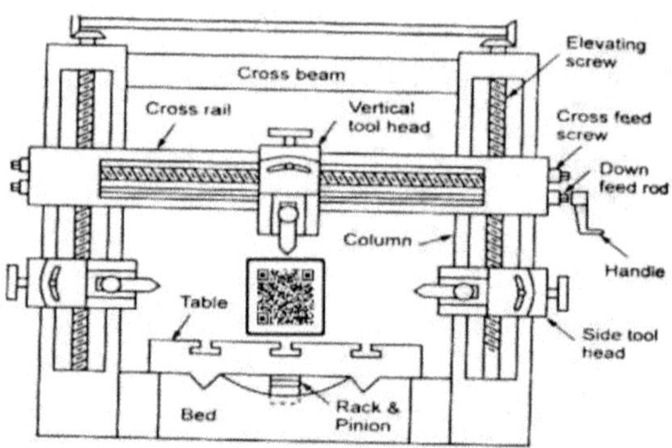

PIT PLANER

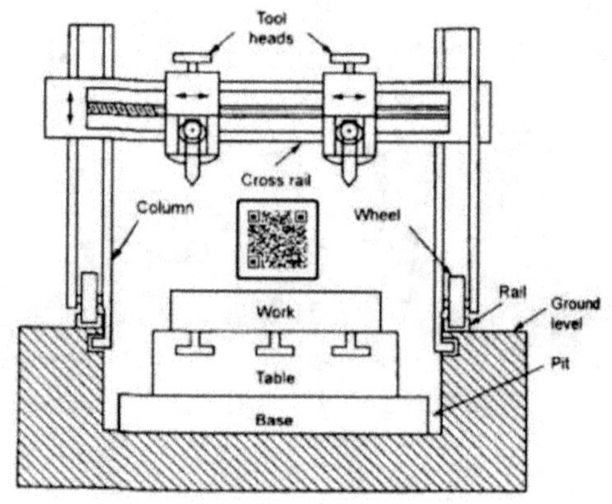

OPEN SIDE PLANER

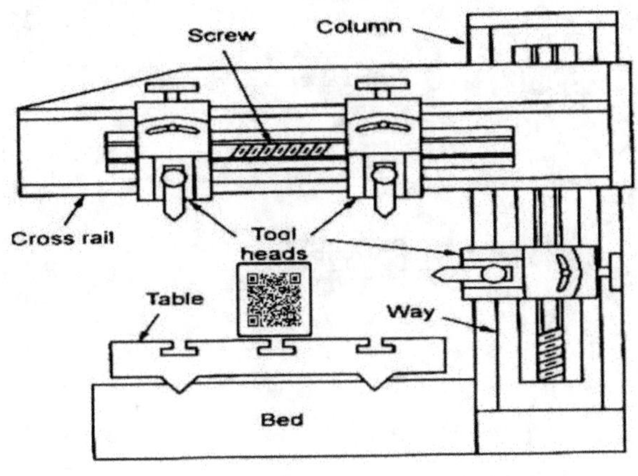

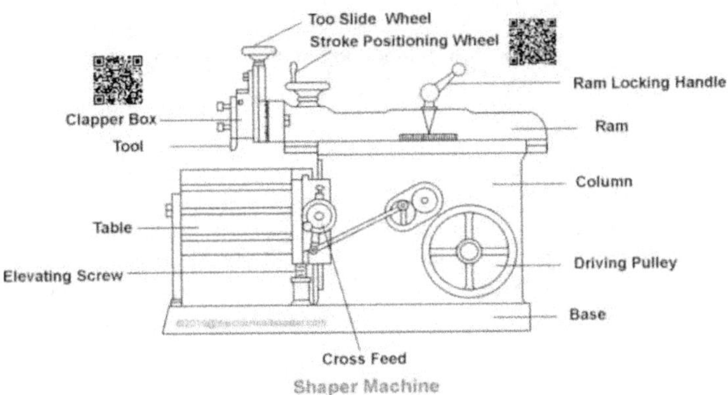

Shaper Machine

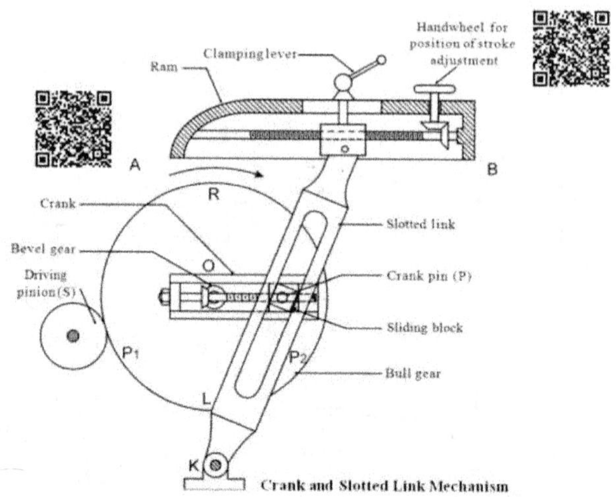

Quick Return Mechanism of Shaper Machine

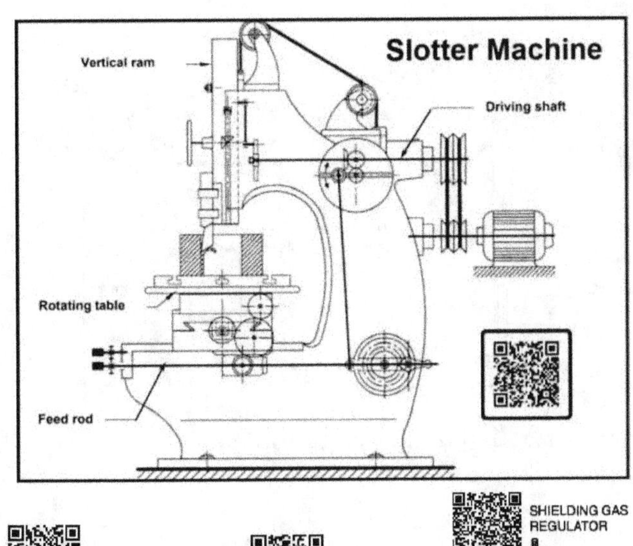

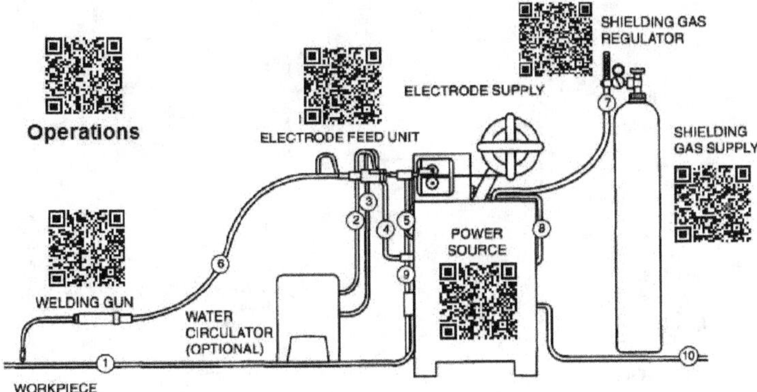

Gas Metal Arc Welding

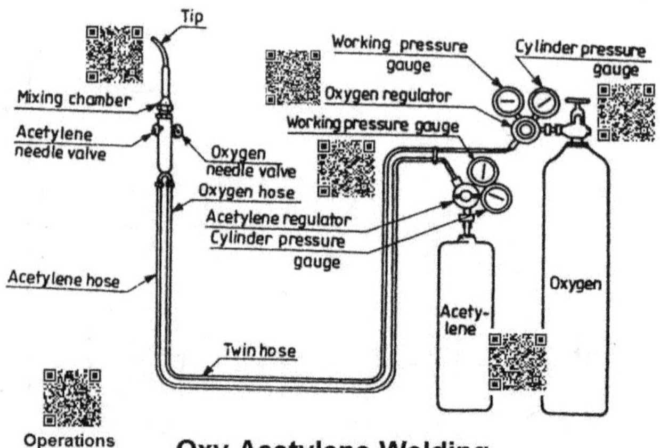

Oxy Acetylene Welding

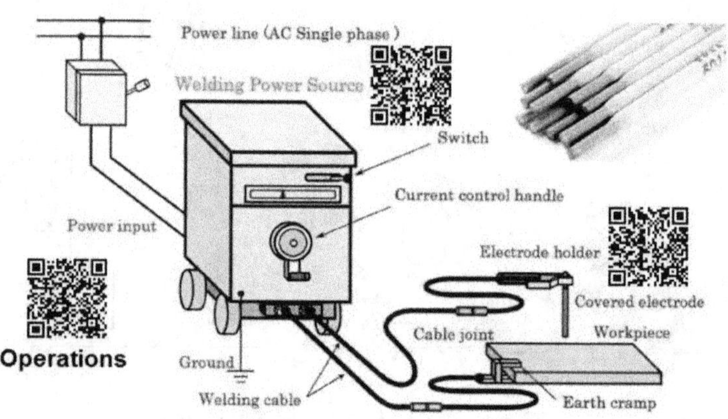

Shielded Metal Arc Welding

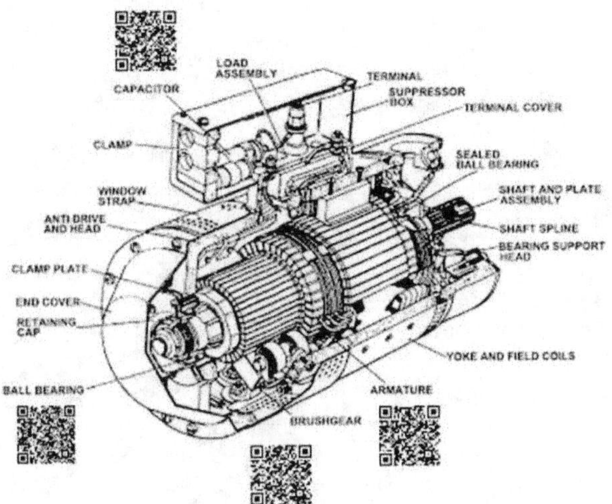

Electrical Generator

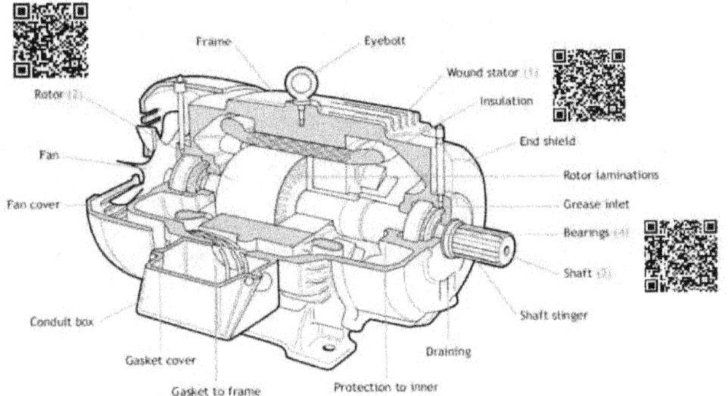

Electrical Induction Motor

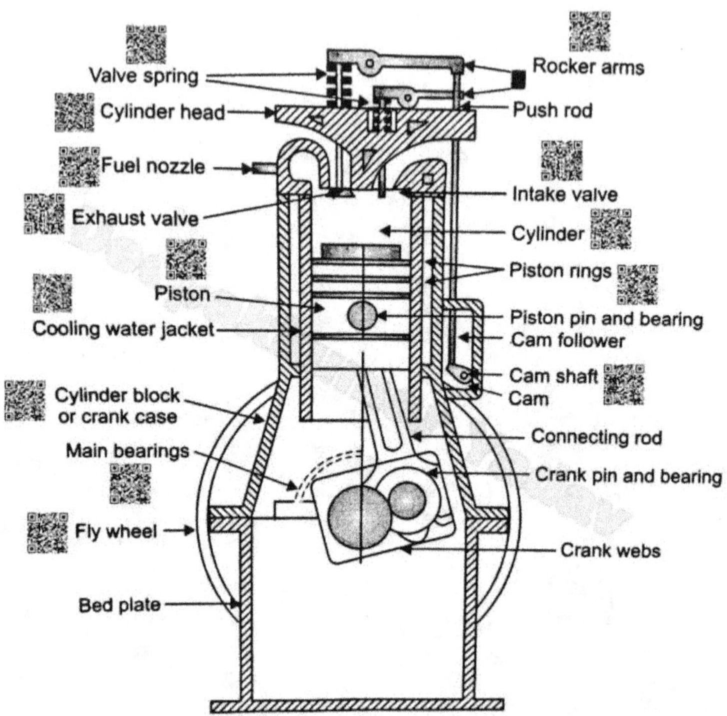

Components of Diesel Engine

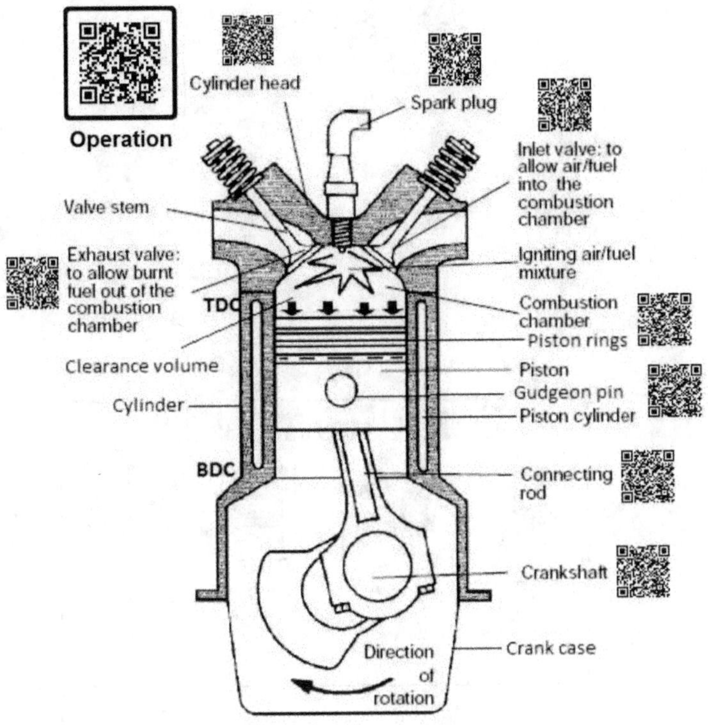

Petrol Engine Details

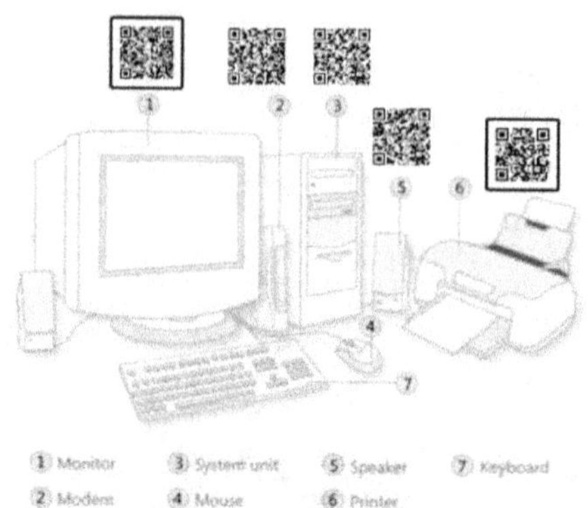

1 Monitor
2 Modem
3 System unit
4 Mouse
5 Speaker
6 Printer
7 Keyboard

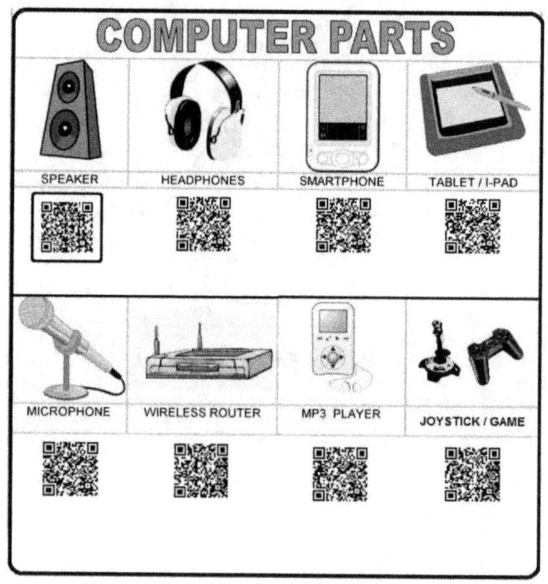

COMPUTER PARTS
SPEAKER
HEADPHONES
SMARTPHONE
TABLET / I-PAD
MICROPHONE
WIRELESS ROUTER
MP3 PLAYER
JOYSTICK / GAME

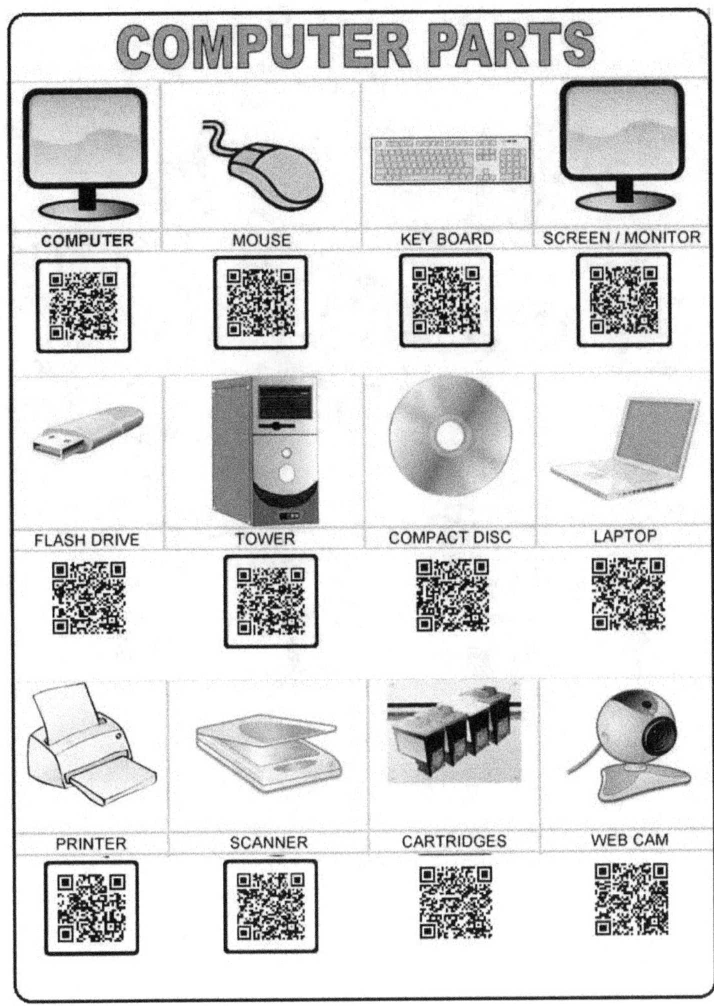
COMPUTER PARTS
COMPUTER
MOUSE
KEY BOARD
SCREEN / MONITOR
FLASH DRIVE
TOWER
COMPACT DISC
LAPTOP
PRINTER
SCANNER
CARTRIDGES
WEB CAM

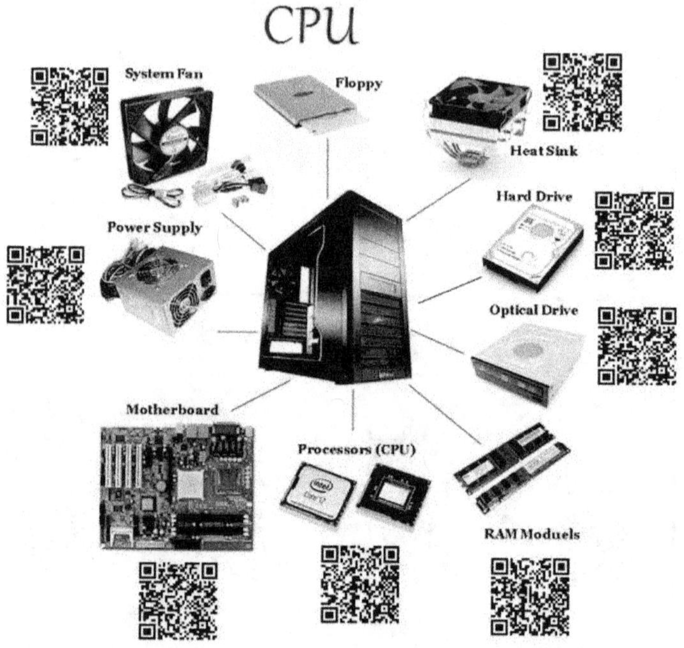

Computer CPU
Hardware Components

Motherboard
Hardware Components

Grinding

Fire extinguisher

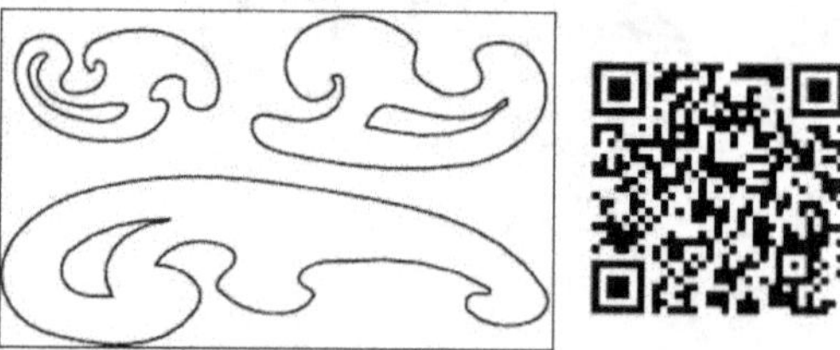

French curve in drawing

Set square in drawing

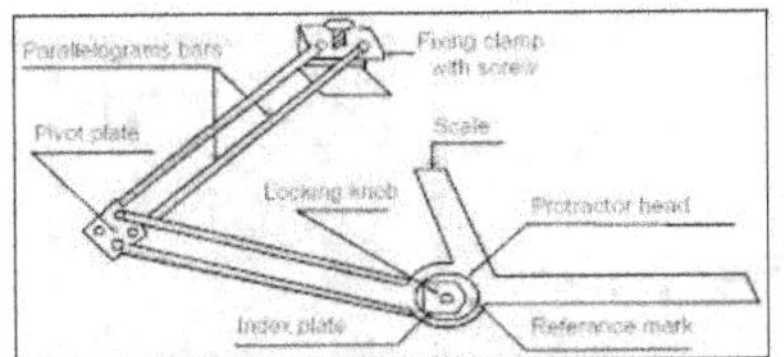

Mini drafter in drawing

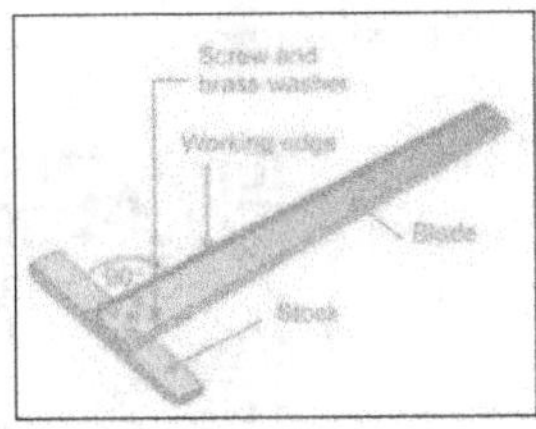

T - square in drawing

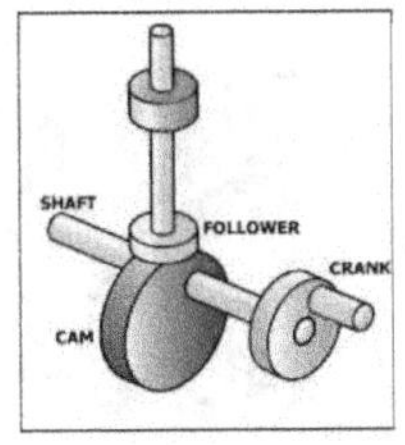

Cams in engine

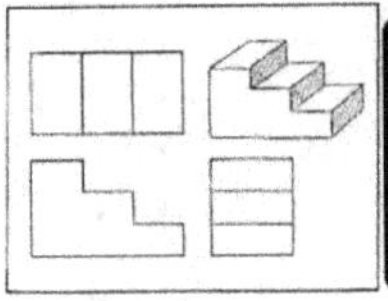

Orthographic projection in drawing

Third angle projection drawing

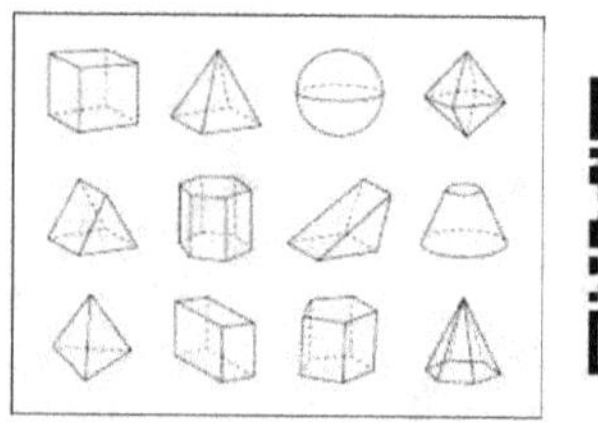

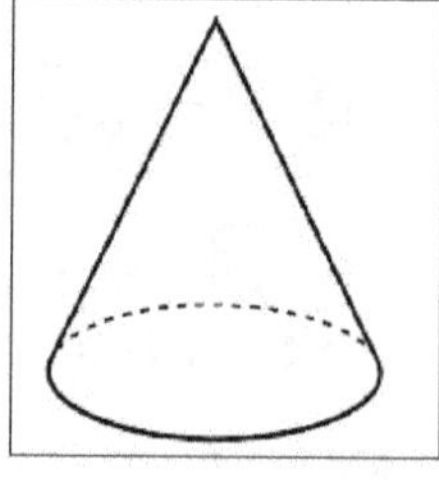

Cone in engineering drawing

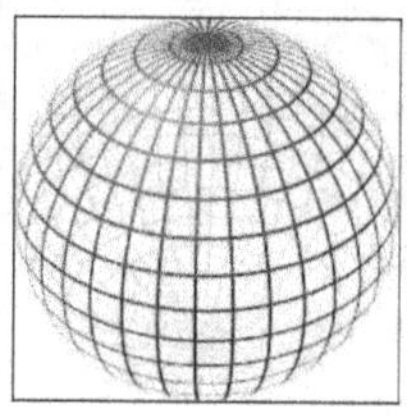

Sphere in drawing

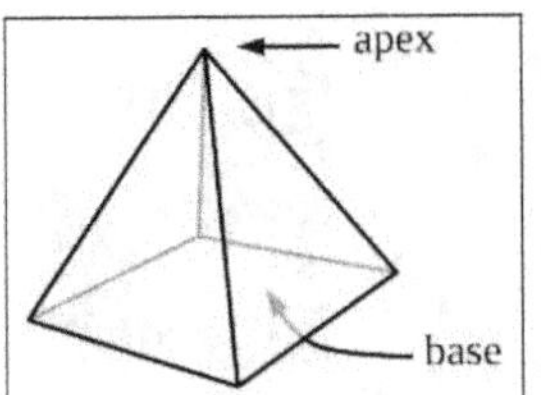

Pyramid drawing

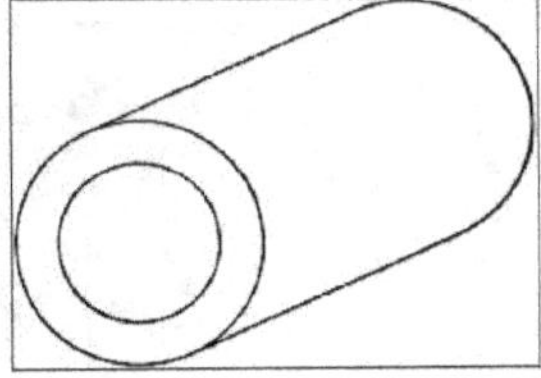

Cylinder in drawing

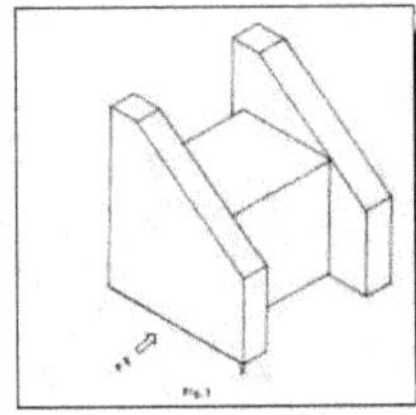

Isometric projections drawing

Curves engineering drawing

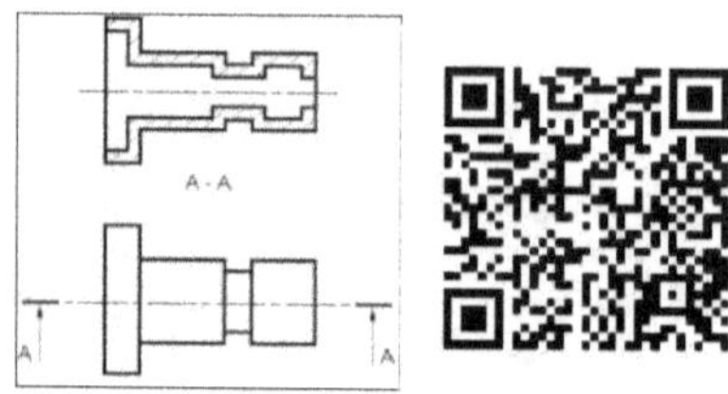

Sectional views in drawing

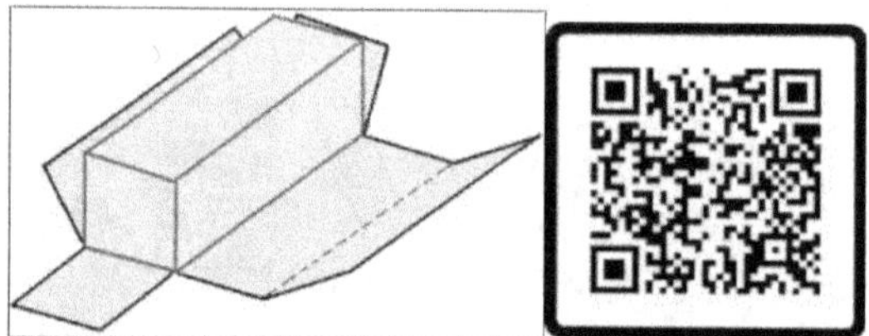

Development of surfaces in drawing

Hexagonal plane in drawing

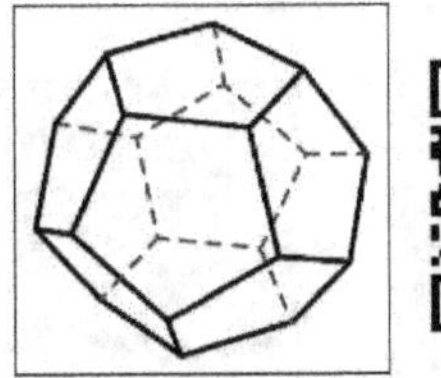

Polyhedron in drawing

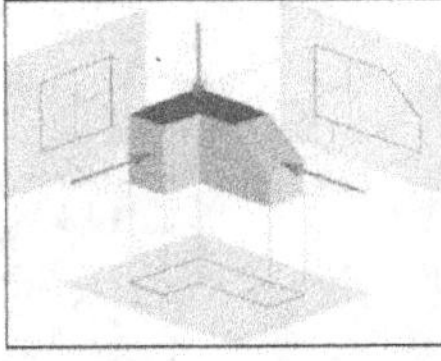

First Angle projection method in drawing

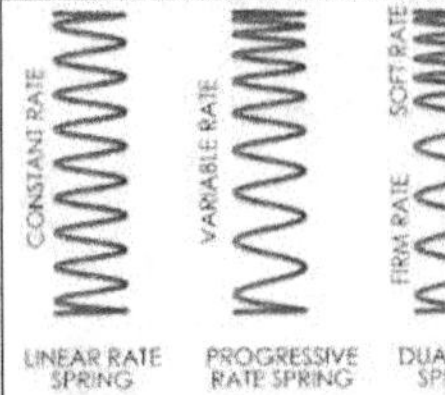

Springs in drawing

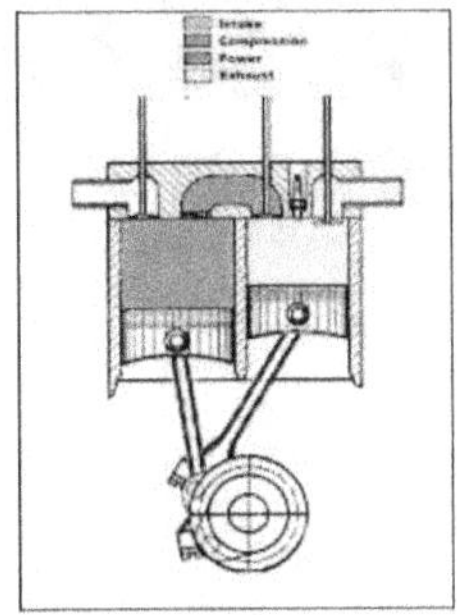

Engine in vehicle

Piston & rings in Engine

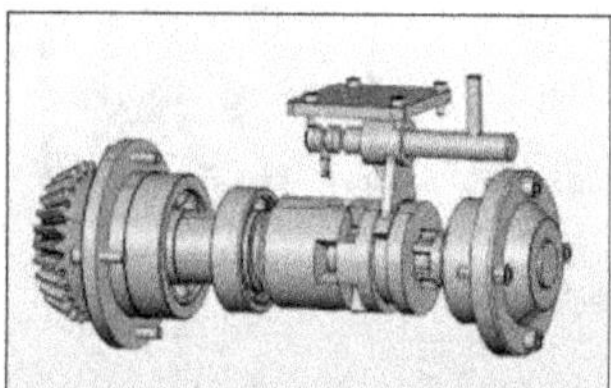

Dog clutches in vehicle

Fire extinguisher

Calliper

Hacksaw frame

Universal surface guage

Hammer

Centre punch

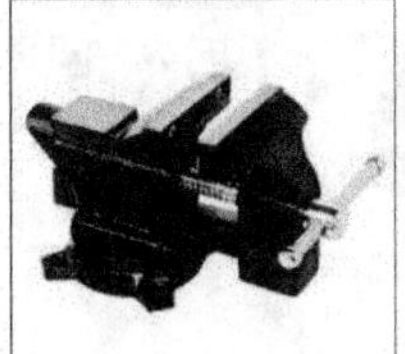

Bench vice

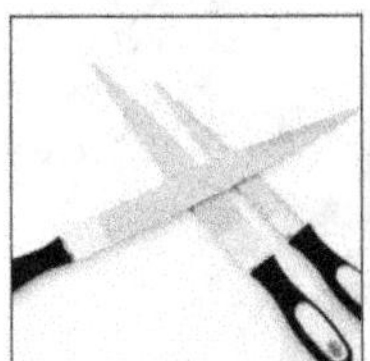

Files

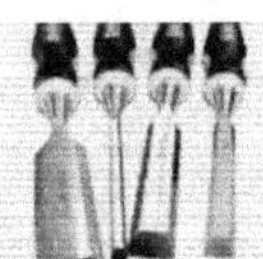

Scraper

Surface Plate

Outside Micrometer

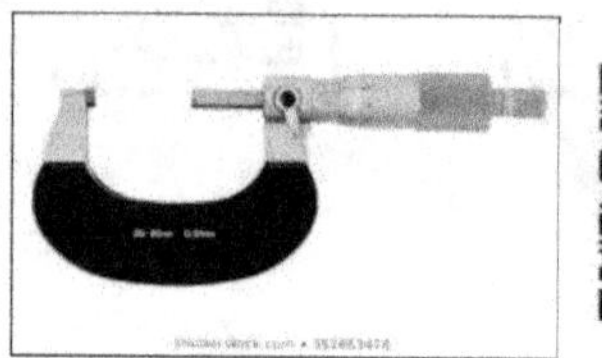

Micrometer

Depth micrometer

Vernier Calliper

Vernier bevel protractor

Drilling

Reamer

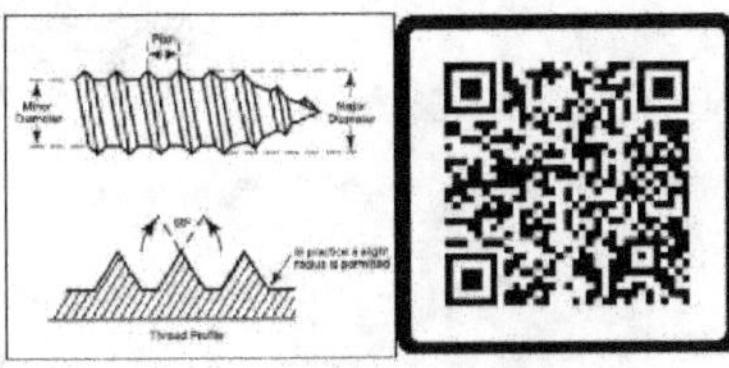

Thread

Tap Die

Grinding Wheel

Slip gauge

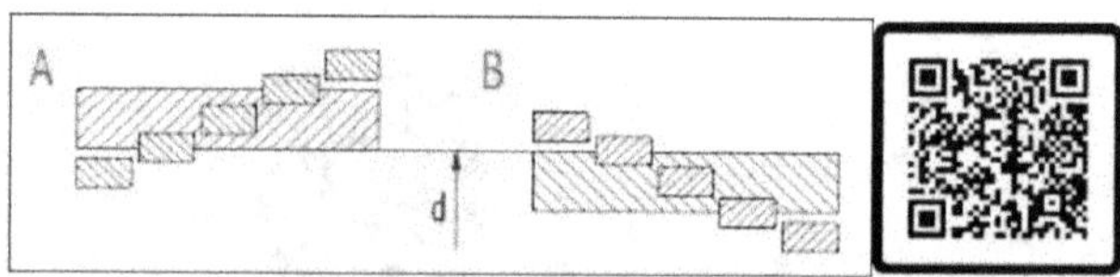

Limit fit tolerance

Lathe Machine

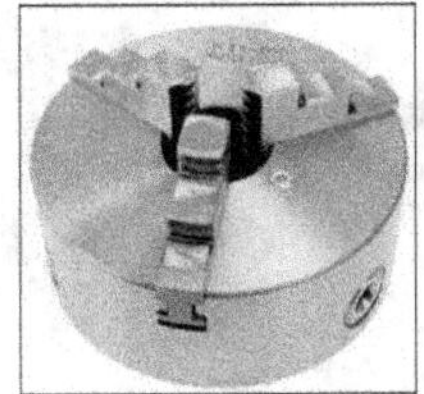

Lathe chuck

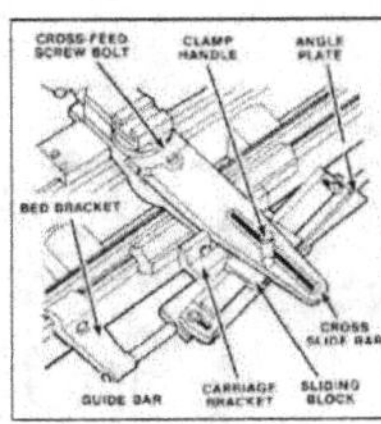

Taper turning attachment

taper ring gauge

screw pitch gauge

Gear

screw pitch gauge

Tap Die

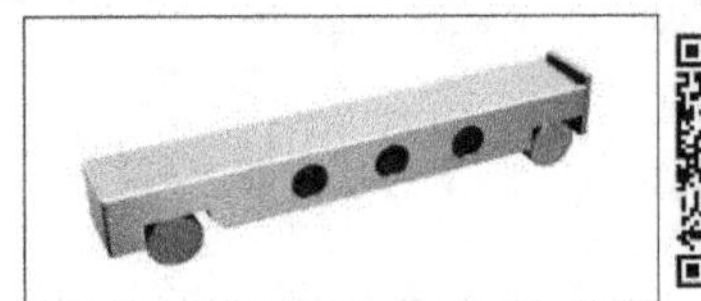

Sine bar

Slip gauge

<u>Dial test indicator</u>

Telescopic gauge

Feeler gauge

Centre gauge

Jig

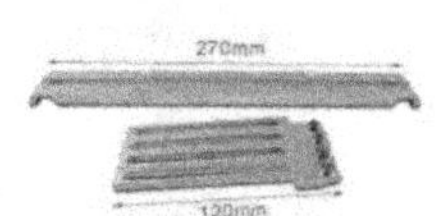

Fixture

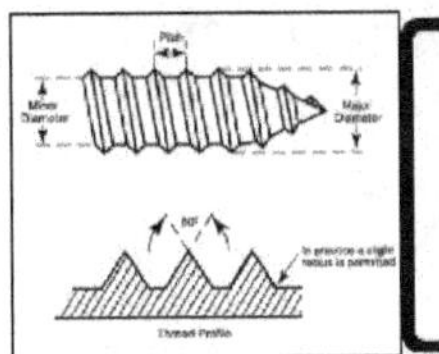

Thread

CHAPTER TWO

Draughtsman Mechanical MCQ

01] In case of bleeding, take treatment Of

D] cold 3" and rest

A] spray cold water

B] Bandage immediately -----.

B] Enquire about the accident thought treatment

02] in case of an accident, the victim should im

A] Asked to take rest

C] Attended immediately

D] leave him

03] First aid is given to an injured or ill person primarily....

A] Save life

B] Prevent further deterioration of the muff's

C] Give best possible comfort

D] All of these

04] Colour code for Bins for waste paper segregation is -----

A] blue Colour

B] Yellow Colour

C] Red Colour

D] Green Colour

05] In Japanese Seiko stands for --------------

A] Shine

B] Sort

C] Standardize

D] Sustain

06] Benefit of SS system is ------

A] Increase in productivity

B] Increase in quality

C] Reduction in wastage of time

D] All of these

07] Safety is -----------

A] nobody's business

B] every bodise business

C] Some bodies business

D] The organization business

08] For basic categories of safety signs are available The meaning of"prohibition" sign ----

A] shows it must not be done

B] Shows what must be done

C] Warns the hazard or danger

D] Gives information of safety provision

09] Which one is a workshop safety?

A] Keep shop floor clean and free from grease, oil or other slippery materials

B] Stop the machine before changing the speed

C] Don't use cracked or chipped tools

D] Don't try to stop a running machine with hand

10] In Personal Protect Equipment (PPE] HELMET is used to

A] protect head

B] Protect eyes

C] Protect hands

D] Protect ears

11] Which of the following belongs to general safety?

A Have a worker in good attitude

B] The work clean and clear

C] Concentrate on your work

D] Keep the floor and gangways clean and clear

12] While grinding, which is used to protect the eyes?

A] Dark green glass

B] Mask

C] Sun glasses

D] Safety goggles

Grinding

13] Which of the following is done for machine safety?

A] Check the oil level before starting the machine

B] Do things in a methodical way

C] Keep the floor and gangways clean and clear

D] Don't use dies and scarves

14] ln Personal Protect Equipment (PPE] , 'sleeves' is used to protect -----------

A] Face

B] Eyes

C] Ears

D] Hands

15] ABC stands for --------------

A] Automatic Breathing Control

B] Automatic Blood Control

C] Airway Breathing Circulation

D] Automatic Blood Circulation

16] To put off"Class B" fire, the types of fire extinguisher used is ....

A] dry power

B] Carbon dioxide

C] Jet of water

D] Foam type

17] Which type of fire extinguisher is used to put off general fire?

A] Water type Extinguisher

B] Foam type Extinguisher

C] Dry chemical powder Extinguisher

D] Carbon dioxide (C02] Extinguisher

Fire extinguisher

18]The 'T' square is used for drawing lines ......

a] inclined

b] curved

c] vertical

d] horizontal

19] For drawing large size circle is drawn by.....

a] straight bar

b] lengthening bar

c] big bar

d] small bar

20] To draw or measure angle is used by.....

a]set square

b] protractor

c] 'T' square

d] none of these

21] The grade of pencil is used to sketching lettering ....

a] conical point

b] chisel point

c] soft

d] low

22] For drawing thin lines of uniform thickness the pencil should be sharpened in the form of ....

a] chisel edge

b]conical

c] pointed

d] none of these

23] What is used for drawing curves which can not drawn by compass

a] small compass

b] French curve

c] protractor

d] none of these

French curve in drawing

24]Unnecessary lines is removed by .....

a] Duster

b] sand paper block

c] <u>eraser</u>

d] none of these

25] Circle and arcs are drawn by means of .....l.

a] <u>compass</u>

b] divider

c] lengthening bar

d]none of these

26] Inking pen is used in drawing ......

a] horizontal line

b] non circular arcs

c] vertrical lines

d] <u>all of these</u>

27] The card board scale are available in set of .....

a] 7

b] 8

c] 6

d] 9

28] The convenient length size of 30 -60°-90° set square for used in school and colleges are......

a] 250

b] 200

c] 300

d] none of these

Set square in drawing

29] Drawing board is shape of ....

a] square

b] rectangular

c] triangular

d] none of these

30] The 'T' square , set square ,scale protractor are complain use in........

a] protractor

b] <u>mini drafter</u>

c] set square

d] none of these

Mini drafter in drawing

31]Set square , T square edges are bevelled for the purpose of....

a] curve line

b] <u>inking lines</u>

b] taking measurements

d] none of these

T - square in drawing

32]Geometrical construction which are mostly based on plane geometry and which are very.......

a] Accuracy

b] Quality

c] <u>Essential</u>

d] Superior quality

33] How much method of drawing the regular polygons.......

a] Inscribe circle method and arc method

b] General method for drawing any polygon

c] Alternative method

d] <u>All of these</u>

34] The line AB can be divided into .... equal parts.

a] <u>Z</u>

b] 10

c] 15

d] All of them

35] Which method of constructing triangl in circle......

a] <u>Inscribing</u>

b] Describing

c] Both a and b

d] None of these

36] When two sides of the hexagon are required to be horizontal the starting point for stepping equal division should be on an end of the.....

a] <u>Horizontal diameter</u>

b] Vertical diameter

c] Inclined diameter

d] None of these

37] If two sides of hexagon are required to be vertical the starting point should be on an end of the....

a] Inclined diameter

b] Horizontal diameter

c] <u>Vertical diameter</u>

d] None of these

38] The section obtained by the inter section of the right circular cone by a plane in different position relative to the axis of the cone are called.......

a] <u>Conics</u>

b] Circles

c] Triangles

d] Half circle

39] When the section plane is inclined to the axis and cuts all the generators on one side on a apex the section is in......

a] Conic section

b] <u>Ellipse</u>

c] Parabola

d] Hyperbola

40] When the section plane is inclined to the axis and is parallel to one of the generators the section is a ....

a] Ellipse

b] <u>Parabola</u>

c] Hyperbola

d] Cycloid

41] Use of elliptical curve is........

a] Arches

b] Dams and monuments

c] Manholes, gland & stuffing boxes

d] <u>All of these</u>

42] Use of parabolic curve is.........

a] Bridges & arches

b] Sound reflectors

c] Light reflectors

d] <u>All of these</u>

43] Use of hyperbolical curve is......

a] <u>Cooling towers and water channel</u>

b] Dames

c] Bridges

d] All of these

44] When the point is within the circle, the curve is called an.......

a] Superior trochoid

b] Interior trochoid

c] Trochoid

d] Isotrochoid

45] When the point outside the circle then the curve is called as......

a] Interior trochoid

b] Superior trochoid

c] Trochoid

d] Insuperior trochoid

46] The curve general by a point on a circumference of a circle, which rolls without slipping along another circle it is called.......

a] Epicycloids

b] Hypocycloid

c] Involute

d] None of these

47] When the circle rolls inside another circle the curve is called.......

a] Hypocycloid

b] Epicycloids

c] Trochoid

d] Hypotrochoid

48] The use of archemedian spiral curve is made in........

a] Teeth profiles of helical gears

b] Profiles of cams

c] Both a & b

d] None of these

Cams in engine

49] The cams are widely used in........

a] Automates

b] Printing machines

c] C engines

d] <u>All of these</u>

50] Spring index =

a] Diameter of coil / diameter of a wire

b] <u>Diameter of wire /diameter of coil</u>

c] Mean diameter of wire / diameter of coil

d] Mean diameter of a coil / diameter of wire

51] Eccentricity =

a] <u>Distance of a point from the focus / distance of the point from directrix</u>

b] Distance of focus from point / distance of point from

c] Distance of point from focus / distance of directrix of point

d] Distance of point from directrix / distance of point from focus

52] Mathematically an ellipse can be described by equation.....

a] $a^2 / X^2 + y^2 / b^2 = 1$

b] $x^2 / a^2 + y^2 / b^2$

c] $x^2 / a^2 + y^2 / b^2 = 0$

d] <u>$x^2 / a^2 + y^2 / b^2 = 1$</u>

53] Mathematically a parabola can be described by an equation......

a] $y^2 = 4ax$

b] $x^2 = 2ay$

c] $x^2 = 4ay$

d] <u>Both a & b</u>

54] Mathematically hyperbola can be described by an equation.......

a] <u>$x^2 /a^2 - y^2 /b^2 = 1$</u>

b] $x^2 /y^2 - y^2 /x^2 = 0$

c] Both a & b

d] None of these

55] Cycloid can be described by an equation......

a] $y = a(1-\cos \emptyset)$

b] $x = a(\emptyset -\sin \emptyset)$

c] <u>Both a & b</u>

d] None of these

56] The mathematically represented hypocycloid is.....

a] $Y = a \cos^3 \emptyset$, $X = a \sin^3 \emptyset$

b] $X = a \sin^3 \emptyset$, $Y = a \cos^3 \emptyset$

c] <u>$X = a \cos^3 \emptyset$, $Y = a \sin^3 \emptyset$</u>

d] None of these

57] Mathematically represented by involute is

a] $X = r \sin \emptyset - r \emptyset \cos \emptyset$, $Y = r \cos + r \emptyset \sin \emptyset$

b] $X = r \sin \emptyset + r \cos \emptyset$, $Y = r \cos \emptyset - r \emptyset \sin \emptyset$

c] $Y = r \emptyset \cos \emptyset - r \sin \emptyset$, $X = r \sin \emptyset - r \emptyset \cos \emptyset$

d] <u>$X = r \cos \emptyset + r \emptyset \sin \emptyset$, $Y = r \sin \emptyset - r \emptyset \cos \emptyset$</u>

58] The lines from the object to the plane are called.......

a] Projection

b] <u>Projector</u>

c] Reference plane

d] None of these

59] The orthographic projection an object is represented by View on the mutual perpendicular projection lines

a] <u>Two or three</u>

b] Three or two

c] Three or four

d] None of these

60] When the projectors are parallel to each other & also perpendicular to the plane, the projection is called......

a] Isometric projection

b] Oblique projection

c] <u>Orthographic projection</u>

d] Perspective projection

Orthographic projection in drawing

61] The two planes employed for the purpose of Orthographic projections are......

a] Auxillary plane

d] Horizontal plane

c] <u>Reference plane</u>

d] None of these

62] The line in which they intersect is termed the reference line & is denoted by the letters.......

a] AB

b] YZ

c] <u>XY</u>

d] None of these

63] The projection on the VP is called........

a] Side view

b] <u>Front view</u>

c] Top view

d] All of these

64] ....Method, when the views are drawn in their relative positions, the plane comes below the elevation. The view of the object as observed from the left-side the right of elevation.

a] Plane of projection

b] <u>First angle projection</u>

c] Third angle projection

d] None of these

65] Third angle projection method, the object is assumed to be situated in the........ quadrant.

a] First quadrant

b] Second quadrant

c] <u>Third quadrant</u>

d] Fourth quadrant

66] .... Method of projection is used in U.S.A & also in other countries.

a] plane of projection

b] Orthographic projection

c] First-angle projection

d] <u>Third angle projection</u>

Third angle projection drawing

67] When an object is situated on the ground, in first angle projection method, the bottom of its ..... will co-inside with XY

a] Top view

b] <u>Front view</u>

c] side view

d] All of these

68] The important element of this projection system

a] An object

b] Plane of projection

c] An observer

d] <u>All of these</u>

69] When line AB is parallel to HP hence ....

a] It' front view to AB

b] It''s side view equal to AB

c] <u>It's top view equal to AB</u>

d] None of these

70] When a line is parallel to a plane; it's projection on plane is equal to it's ;

a] <u>True length</u>

b] True shape

c] True size

d] None of these

71] The point is parallel in which the line or line produced meet the point is plane is called it's ....

a] Line

b] ratio

c] <u>Trace</u>
d] none of these
72] .... is the shortest distance between two points.
a] a line
b] a point
c] <u>a straight line</u>
d] none of these
73] When the line intersect horizontal plane that's called.....
a] <u>horizontal trace</u>
b] vertical trace
c] trace of line
d] none of these
74]Planes may be divided into two main types ......
a] Perpendicular planes, auxillary planes
b] <u>Perpendicular plane, oblique planes</u>
c] Auxillary planes , perpendicular planes
d] none of these
75] Planes which are inclined to the reference plane are called......
a] Auxillary plane
b] <u>obliqeu plane</u>
c] Perpendicular planes
d] picture plane
76] When a plane is perpendicular to a reference plane it's projection on that plane is a..........
a] horizontal line
b] parallel line
c] <u>straight line</u>
d] none of these
77] When a plane is parallel to a reference plane , it's projection on that plane shows........
a] <u>It's true shape &size</u>
b] It's true length & size
c] It's true height & size
d] none of these
78] Plane perpendicular to VP & HP that plane is called as ....
a] Auxillary Plane
b] Oblique Plane
c] <u>Perpendicular Plane</u>

d] None of these
79] Perpendicular plane can be divides into the following types.........
a] Perpendicular to both the reference planes.
b] Perpendicular to one plane & parallel to other
c] Perpendicular to one plane & inclined to other
d] <u>All of these</u>
80] The planes have only two dimensions, viz........
a] <u>Length & breadth</u>
b] Length & height
c] Length & thickness
d] All of these
81] The imaginary line of prism joining the centrs of the bases called.........
a] Faces
b] <u>Axis</u>
c] Apex
d] Base
82] A right & regular prism has it's axis....... to the bases
a] Parallel
b] <u>Perpendicular</u>
c] Inclined
d] None of these

83] When a pyramid or a cone is cut by a plane parallel to it's base thus removing the top portion, the remaining portion is called it's.........
a] Sphere
b] Cone
c] Cylinder
d] <u>Frustum</u>

Cone in engineering drawing

84] Oblique cylinder & cones have their axes........ to their base

a] <u>Inclined</u>

b] Parallel

c] Perpendicular

d] All of these

85] Projection of two equal sphere s resting on the ground & in contact with each other, with the line joining there centre parallel to the..........

a] A VP

b] VP

c] <u>HP</u>

d] All of these

Sphere in drawing

86] Projections of section on the other plane to which it is inclined is called.......

a] Section planes

b] <u>Apparent section</u>

c] True shape of sphere

d] None of these

87] When the section plane is parallel to the HP or the ground, the true shape of the section will be seen in.........

a] Front view

b] Side view

c] <u>Top view</u>

d] All of these

88] Surface of solid are laid out on a plane the figure obtained is called its........

a] Interpenetration

b] <u>Development</u>

c] Intersection

d] None of these

89] Development of surfaces is essential in.........

a] Foundry shop

b] <u>Sheet metal work</u>

c] Fitting shop

d] None of these

90] Which method of development used in transition pieces?

a] Parallel diameter

b] Radial line method

c] <u>Triangulation method</u>

d] Approximate method

91] Which method of development used in pyramids and cones.........

a] <u>Radial line method</u>

b] Parallel line method

c] Approximate method

d] Triangulation method

Pyramid drawing

92] Parallel line method is used in..........

a] Prism

b] Cylinder

c] Cubes

d] <u>All of these</u>

93] Which method of development used in surface as sphere, paraboloid, ellipsoid, hyperboloid, and helicoids

a] Radial line method

b] Triangulation method

c] <u>Approximate method</u>

d] Parallel line method

94] Zone method and lune method is used in development of........

a] Prisms

b] Cones

c] <u>Sphere</u>

d] Pyramids

95] Calculation the subtended angle Θ by the formula $\Theta = 360^0 \times$ radius of the base circle

a] <u>Length of axis</u>

b] <u>Slant height</u>

c] Radius of axis

d] None of these

96] In engineering practice, objects constructed may have constituent part, the surfaces of which intersect one another in lines called........ of intersection.

a] <u>Lines</u>

b] Cones

c] Cylinder

d] Prisms

97] The line of interaction may be depending upon the nature of.......

a] <u>Intersection surface</u>

b] Intersecting solids

c] Intersection cones

d] None of these

98] The two plane surface intersect in a........ line

a] Curve

b] <u>Straight</u>

c] Plane

d] All of these

99] The line of intersection between two curved surface or between......... Surface and a curved surface is a curve.

a] A curved

b] <u>A plane</u>

c] A solids

d] None of these

100] When a solids completely penetration another solids there will be two lines of intersection. These lines are sometimes called the line or........

a] Line of interpenetration

b] <u>Curve of interpenetration</u>

c] Solids of interpenetration

d] All of these

101] Use of penetration curve is.......

a] Sheet metal work

b] Fitting shop

c] <u>Fabricating work</u>

d] Foundry shop

102] Methods of determining the line of intersection between surface of two interpenetration.........

a] Approximate method & radial line method

b] <u>Line method and cutting plane method</u>

c] Triangulation method and parallel line method

d] None of these

103] Example of interpenetration is..........

a] Two prism intersection

b] Cylinder and prism intersection

c] Cone and cylinders intersection

d] <u>All of these</u>

104] Two cylinder intersection is example of.........

a] <u>Intersection</u>

b] Interpenetration

c] Cone intersection

d] None of these

Cylinder in drawing

105] .... Method is explained in detail while solving illustrative problems

a] Line method

b] Radial line method

c] <u>Cutting plane method</u>

d] Parallel line method

106] What is a type of isometric projection?

a] <u>Pictorial projection</u>

b] Orthographic projection

c] Perspective projection

d] Oblique Projection

Isometric projections drawing

107] Isometric views have been drawn........

a] Full scale

b] Half scale

c] <u>True length</u>

d] True scale

108] The line parallel to isometric axis are called........

a] Isometric axis

b] <u>Isometric line</u>

c] Isometric planes

d] Isometric views

109] The isometric projection is reduce in the ratio.........

a] 3 :

b] 1 : 2

c] 2 : 2

d] <u>2 : 3</u>

110] The isometric projection of circle drawn with........

a] Isometric Plane

b] Isometric graph

c] Isometric Drawing

d] <u>Isometric Scale</u>

111] The major axis of the ellipse is long than...............

a] Radius of the circle

b] True diameter

c] <u>Diameter of the circle</u>

d] None of these

112] Makes practice for drawing of isometric view using........

a] Isometric planes

b] Isometric lines

c] <u>Isometric graph</u>

d] Isometric view

113] Use of parabolic curve is

a] <u>Sound reflectors</u>

b] Dams

c] Man hole of boiler

d] Gland & stuffing box

Curves engineering drawing

114] When the section plane is inclined the true shape of section on

a] AVP

b] VP

c] HP

d] <u>A/P</u>

115] When section plane is perpendicular to both the HP & VP the true shape of section on

a]Top view

b] <u>Side view</u>

c] Front view

d]None of this

116] When view projected on auxiliary planes are called

a] <u>Auxiliary view</u>

b Sectional view

c] Front view

d] None of these

117] Invisible features of an object are shown by means of

a] Outline

b] Chain lines

c] <u>Hidden lines</u>

d] None of these

118] Importance of sectional view on drawing for

a] <u>Internal details</u>

b] Outer details

c] Hatching

d] None of these

Sectional views in drawing

119] The component is cut by a straight cutting plane is divided in to two parts

a] Half section

b] <u>Full section</u>

c] Offset section

d] Removed section

120] section line is two different parts (pieces] in contact should be drown in...

a] Same direction

b] <u>Opposite direction</u>

c]parallel direction

d] None of these

121] When area to be sectioned in very small as for this plate and structural members blacked in section may be used. A space of not less than

a] 0.07mm

b] <u>0.7mm</u>

c] 0.05mm

d] 0.5mm

122] The sum of interior angles of polygon is equal

a] <u>(2*n-4]*Right angle</u>

b] (2*n]*Right angle-4

c] (2*4-n]*Right angle

d] (2-4*n]*Right angle

123] One micron is equal to ....mm

a] <u>0.001</u>

b] 1000

c] 0.01

d] 0.1

124] Development of surface is essential in.....

a] foundry shop

b] <u>sheet metal work</u>

c] fitting shop

d] none of these

Development of surfaces in drawing

125] Which method of development used in transition piece?

a] parallel line method

b] radial line method

c] <u>triangulation method</u>

d] none of these

126] The isometric projection is reduced in the ratio of

a] √2:√3

b] √3:√2

c] 1:√2

d] <u>none of these</u>

127] When measurements are required in three units the scale is used....

a] full scale
b] plain scale
c] half scale
d] none of these
128]Isometric drawing is larger in production about isometric projection is....
a] 22.5%
b] 0.815
c] 9/11
d] none of these
129] While isometric of sphere of spherical parts.......is must be used.
a] full scale
b] isometric length
c] true length
d] half scale
130] When circle draw with isometric scale the length of major axis of the ellipse to the ....
a] true diameter
b] isometric diameter
c] isometric diameter
d] none of these
131] In isometric view which contain a large number of non –isometric lines which method is used
a] box method
b] off-set method
c] co-ordinate method
d] centre lay out method
132] When drawing is drawn smaller than actual size of object .....
a] full scale
b] enlarging scale
c] reducing scale
d] none of these
133] When e=1 curve is called.....
a] parabola
b] hyperbola
c] ellipse
d] none of these

134]Compare with isometric drawing the advantage of oblique projection is....

a] <u>front face is in true shape</u>

b] two axis are always perpendicular to each othe

c] receding axis is taken at some convenient angles

d] none of these

135]If all the receding edges are drawn true length the oblique projection is called...

a] <u>cavilier projection</u>

b] cabinet projection

c] general projection

d] none of these

136] The large object such as building the point is usually taken height of .....

a] 0.8mm

b] 1.2mm

c] <u>1.8mm</u>

d] 1.5mm

137] Central plane is the imaginary vertical plane which passes through....

a] <u>P. P</u>

b] H.L

c] G.P

d] C.P

138] When object is parallel to P.P the perspective is called......

a] <u>one point</u>

b] two point

c] three point

d] none of these

139] The line drawn through the station point from the picture plane shall be ....

a] <u>P.A</u>

b] H.L

c] G.L

d] C

140] The distance of the station point from the picture plane shall be .....

a] Max. Diameter of the object

b] <u>Twice the max. Diameter of the object</u>

c] Half the max. Diameter of the object
d] none of these
141] In isometric view of hexagonal plane all the sides of hexagon is .....
a] equal length
b] <u>unequal length</u>
c] none of these

Hexagonal plane in drawing
142] When all the faces are equal & regular the polyhedron is said....
a] <u>regular</u>
b] prisms
c] irregular
d] pyramid

Polyhedron in drawing
143] Oblique prisms & pyramid have ......
a] axis perpendicular to the base
b] <u>axis inclined to the base</u>
c] faces inclined to the H.P
d] none of these

144] Icosahedrons has equal equilateral triangular faces
a] 12
b] 8
c] <u>20</u>
d] 6

145] When a pyramid or cone is cut by a plane parallel to its base is called.....
a] pyramid
b] turned carted
c] <u>frustum</u>
d] none of these

146] Plane which are inclined to both the reference plane is called ......
a] <u>oblique plane</u>
b] perpendicular plane
c] inclined plane
d] none of these

147] When a line parallel to H.P & perpendicular to V.P the trace line is.....
a] <u>V.T</u>
b] H.T
c] no trace
d] V.T& H.T

148] When a line parallel to the V.P and inclined to H.P the true length of line in.....
a] <u>front view</u>
b] top view
c] side view
d] none of these

149] When point situated in front quadrant
a] above the H.P & in front of V.P
b] <u>below the H.P & in front of V.P</u>
c] behind the V.P & above H.P
d] below the H.P & behind the V.P

150] Find the quadrant of point "b" is 15 mm above H.P and 25mm behind the V.P
a] I st
b] III rd
c] IIII th

d] <u>II nd</u>

151] In first angle projection front view is ......

a] <u>above the top view</u>

b] below the top view

c] above the side view

d] below the side view

First Angle projection method in drawing

152] In orthographic projection the projectors are ....

a] parallel to plane

b] <u>perpendicular to plane</u>

c] inclined to plane

d] none of these

153] L.H.S.V means.........

a] length of side view

b] left hand view

c] right hand view

d] <u>left hand side view</u>

154] The object lines between the observer and the plane of projection is ....

a] 3rd angle

b] <u>1st angle</u>

c] 4th angle

d] 2nd angle

155] In third angle projection plane of projection is assumed to be ......

a] non transparent

b] quadrant

c] <u>transparent</u>

d] dihedral angle

156] In third angle projection top view is always on......

a] <u>above front view</u>
b] above top view
c] below the front view
d] below the side view
157] Four quadrants which may be called as......
a] anticlockwise
b] first and third angle
c] <u>dihedral angles</u>
d] none of these
158] In first angle projection method the view see from the left is placed on .....
a] left of the front view
b] <u>right of front view</u>
c] above the top view
d] below the front view
159] The size of A2 paper is .....
a] 297*420
b] 594*841
c] <u>420*594</u>
d] 210*297
160] The edge of board on which 'T' square is sli9ding is called ......
a] straight edge
b] <u>working edge</u>
c] chisel edge
d] none of these
161] The size of title block as recommended by B.I.S . is .....
a] <u>185*65</u>
b] 150*50
c] 170*65
d] none of these
162] For A2 size sheet the number of zones suggested by B.I.S. along the length & width.......
a] 12,8
b] 16,12
c] 8,6
d] none of these
163] The drawing sheet is so folded that...... is always on the top.
a] drawing

b] lettering
c] title block
d] none of these
164] In free hand sketching horizontal lines are sketched from.......
a] right to left
b] up to down
c] left to right
d] none of these
165] When drawing is down smaller than actual size of object
a] enlarging scale
b] reducing scale
c] full scale
d] none of these
166] The ratio of the length of the object represented on drawing to the actual length of object is called.......
a] full scale
b] R.F.
c] half scale
d] plain scale
167] When measurements are required in three unit the scale is used.....
a] full scale
b] half scale
c] plain scale
d] none of these
168] When protractor is not available the scale of chord is used ......
a] measure length
b] measure angle
c] measure scale
d] none of these
169] The least count of a vernier calliper is ....
a] 0.001
b] 0.02
c] 0.001
d] 0.0002
170] Which scale is used to read a very small unit with great accuracy?
a] plain scale
b] diagonal scale
c] scale of chord

d] vernier scale

171] The R.F. is greater than one (1] the scale is ....

a] plain scale

b] diagonal scale

c] <u>enlarging scale</u>

d] reducing scale

172] The difference of one primary division and one vernier division is called......

a] <u>least count</u>

b] primary scale

c] vernier scale

d] R.F.

173] One micron is equal to in mm........

a] 1000mm

b] <u>0.001mm</u>

c] 0.01mm

d] 100mm

174] the top surface joining the two sides of adjacent thread is called

<u>A] Crest</u>

B] Root

C] Flank

D] Thread is angle

175] The included angle of the ISO metric thread is --------

A] 27 1 /2°

B] 30°

C] 55°

<u>D] 60°</u>

176] Which one of the following screw thread forms has an included angle of 55° between the flanks of threads?

<u>A] B. A. Thread</u>

B] Acme thread

C] Buttress threads

D] Knuckle thread

177] Which one of the following is used only for finishing and maintaining correct form of thread?

<u>A] Tap</u>

B] Threading tool

C] Threading chaser

D] Tipped tool

Tap Die

178] The angle 0f lS thread (V shaped] is ----------

A] 29°

B] 47 1/4°

C] 50°

D] 60

179] ln which of the following methods, only external threads are made --------

A] Form tool mEthOd

B] Compound rest method

C] Tailstock offset method

D] Taper turning attachment method.

180] The surface joining the crest and the root of a thread is known as ----

A] Flank

B] Shank

C] Pitch surface

D] All Of these

181] Pitch of a two start thread is 4 mm. Then the lead of the thread is given by -----

A] 4mm

B] 2mm

C] 8mm

D] 6mm

182] The Gear ratio required for cutting a screw thread of 2.5 mm on a lathe having a lead screw pitch using single point cutting tool is ----

A] 1:2

B] 2:1

C] 1:1 mm

183] The bottom surface joining the two sides of adjacent thread (external thread] is...

A] Flank

B] <u>Root</u>

C] Crest

D] Pitch

184] The form of thread used in carpenters vice is...

A] Square

B] Acme thread

C] <u>Sawtooth Thread</u>

D] Knuckle thread

185] What is the angle of pipe thread?

A] 60°

B] 47'/2°

C] 29°

D] <u>55°.</u>

186] What is the use of pipe thread?

A] transmission

B] maintain pressure

C] <u>airtight connections</u>

D] none of the above.

187] What is the depth of the 2" pipe thread?

A] 0.5"

B] 0.640"

C] 0.335"

D] <u>0.580".</u>

188] External Thread provide on Rod or Pipe , by Die and Cutting Tool is called ......

(A) Tapping

(B) Dieing

(C) <u>Threading</u>

(D) Grooving

189] Used where bolt and threads are to be protected from damage.

A] <u>Donald cap nut</u>

B] Thumb nut

C] Hexagonal nut

D] Wing-nut

190] Used where frequent removal and fixing is required.
A] Donald cap nut
B] Thumb nut
C] Hexagonal nut
D] <u>Wing-nut</u>
191] Used in machine building and structure work.
A] Donald cap nut
B] Thumb nut
C] <u>Hexagonal nut</u>
D] Wing-nut
192] Used where frequent adjustments are to be made.
A] Donald cap nut
B] <u>Thumb nut</u>
C] Hexagonal nut
D] Wing-nut
193] Nylon inserts in the nut prevent loosening.
A] Locking plate
B] Wire lock
C] <u>Self-locking nut</u>
D] Sawn nut
194] A slot is cut halfway across the nut.
A] Locking plate
B] Wire lock
C] Self-locking nut
D] <u>Sawn nut</u>
195] Prevents slackening of two bolts.
A] Locking plate
B] <u>Wire lock</u>
C] Self-locking nut
D] Sawn nut
196] Prevents rotation of the top nut.
A] <u>Lock-nut</u>
B] Grooved nut
C] Self-locking nut
D] Sawn nut
197] Prevents loosening of nut by the use of a plate shaped to fit the nut.
A] <u>Locking plate</u>
B] Wire lock

C] Self-locking nut

D] Sawn nut

198] Hexagonal nut with the lower part made cylindrical and the recessed groove.

A] Lock-nut

B] Grooved nut

C] Self-locking nut

D] Sawn nut

199] Filling up of the gap be» tween the bottom of the machine and the top of the floor or foundation block.

A] Wooden forms

B] Foundation bolts

C] Grouting

D] Template

200] Used to prevent any movement when the concrete is poured.

A] Wooden forms

B] Foundation bolts

C] Grouting

D] Template

201] Used to hold down the machine firmly on the foundation to prevent it from moving.

A] Wooden forms

B] Foundation bolts

C] Grouting

D] Template

202] Wooden patterns which represents the base of the machine and support bolts over the excavation.

A] Wooden forms

B] Foundation bolts

C] Grouting

D] Template

203] After placing this in the excavation it is firmly braced from the outside to withstand the pressure of concrete.

A] Wooden forms

B] Foundation bolts

C] Grouting

D] Template

204] Used to check the level of the machine

A] Crowbar

B] <u>Spirit level</u>

C] Levelling jacks

D] Wedge

205] For welding a lap fillet joint in vertical position by gas what should be the angle of below pipe to the line of weld?

A] 30° to 40°

B] 45°to 50°

C] 60° to 70°

D] <u>75° to 80°</u>

206] On which of the following factors, the choice of flux for gas welding depend?

A] <u>type of material to be joined</u>

B] type of edge penetration

C] type of fuel gas

D] type of flame used

207] The type of edge preparation done for gas welding a 4mm thick copper butt joint is...

A] single bevel

B] <u>single V</u>

C] double V

D] square

208] The size of nozzle used to gas weld 3.15 mm thick aluminium butt joint is...

A] 13

B] 10

C] 7

D] <u>5</u>

209] The angle of vee groove of a single vee but joint for cast iron welding is...

A] 60°

B] 70°

C] 80°

D] <u>90°</u>

210] For transmitting very low torque.

A] Feather key

B] Gib head key

C] Woodruff key

D] <u>Saddle key</u>

211] Profile of key tends to weaken the shaft.

A] Feather key

B] Gib head key

C] <u>Woodruff key</u>

D] Saddle key

212] For transmitting unidirectional torque.

A] <u>Feather key</u>

B] Gib head key

C] Woodruff key

D] Saddle key

213] For transmitting heavy torque.

A] Feather key

B] <u>Gib head key</u>

C] Woodruff key

D] Saddle key

214] For transmitting very high torque of the impact type in both directions of rotation.

A] Gib head key

B] Woodruff key

C] Saddle key

D] <u>Tangential key</u>

215] Permits sliding or axial movement of the mat« ing piece on the shaft.

A] <u>Feather key</u>

B] Gib head key

C] Woodruff key

D] Saddle key

216] Can be withdrawn easily.

A] Feather key

B] <u>Gib head key</u>

C] Woodruff key

D] Saddle key

217] G.l. pipes are provided externally with

A] no threads

B] <u>parallel threads</u>

C] tapered threads

D] neither parallel nor tapered threads.

218] in the pipe assembly, the hemp packing is used

A] for easy engagement

B] to fill the gap between threads

C] to avoid leakage

D] to get tight fitting.

219] The sealing compound shall be applied on the pipe threads

A] before hemp packing

B] after hemp packing

C] before and after temp packing

D] none of the above.

220] Used on finished tubular wrench surfaces to avoid marking.

A Stillson pipe

B] Chain wrench

C] Strap wrench

D] Footprint wrench

221] Used for gripping and turning pipes and round stocks in confined places.

A] Stillson pipe

B] Chain wrench

C] Strap wrench

D] Footprint wrench

222] Used for holding iarge diameter pipes.

A] Stillson pipe

B] Chain wrench

C] Strap wrench

D] Footprint wrench

223] Used for gripping and turning pipes,tubes and cylindricai rods.

A] Stillson pipe

B] Chain wrench

C] Strap wrench

D] Footprint wrench

224] Secures rope to small pipe or rim.

A] Slip knot

B] Bowline knot

C] Square knot

D] Sheep shank knot.

225] It can be folded and carried to any place. Similar to the quick releasing type pipe vice.

A Portable folding pipe vice

B] Chain pipe vice

C] Pipe vice

D] None of above

226] Used to hold pipes more than 63mm to 200mm diameter.

A] Portable folding pipe vice

B] Chain pipe vice

C] Pipe vice

D] None of above

227] Used for quick holding and locating pipes. Used to hold pipes up to 63mm diameter.

A] Portable folding pipe vice

B] Chain pipe vice

C] Pipe vice

D] None of above

228] Provides deviation of 90°

A] Plug

B] Elbow

C] Bend

D] Reducer 'T' branczh

229] Provides change of direction with a long radius at right angle.

A] Plug

B] Elbow

C] Bend

D] Reducer 'T' branczh

230] Used for closing a line which has an internal thread.

A] Plug

B] Elbow

C] Bend

D] Reducer 'T' branczh

231] Provides deviation of '45°

A] Bend

B] Reducer 'T' branczh

C] Elbow

D] Tee piece

232] Provides outlet at right angles to the run.

A] Bend

B] Reducer 'T' branczh

C] Elbow

D] <u>Tee piece</u>

233] Used where a change in ' pipe diameter is required.

A] Bend

B] <u>Reducer 'T' branczh</u>

C] Elbow

D] Tee piece

234] Selection of a former depends on the

A] <u>outside diameter of the pipe</u>

B] wall thickness of the pipe

C] bore diameter of the pipe

D] all the above.

235] A branch type hand operated pipe bending machine is used to bend

A] P.V.C.pipes

B] onduit pipes

C] <u>G.I.pipes</u>

D] copper pipes.

236] The inner formers of a hydraulic pipe bending machine are able to bend pipes up to a diameter of

A] 40mm

B] 100mm

C] 20mm

D] <u>75mm</u>

237] Rivets for Joining sheets to thick plates.

A] <u>Countersunk head</u>

B] Flat head

C] Pan head

D] Mushroom

238] Rivets for Joining sheet metal.

A] Countersunk head

B] <u>Flat head</u>

C] Pan head

D] Mushroom

239] Rivets for Heavy fabrication work.

A] Countersunk head

B] Flat head

C] <u>Pan head</u>

D] Mushroom

240] Rivets for Reduces the height of rivet head above the meta\ surface

A] Countersunk head

B] Flat head

C] Pan head

D] <u>Mushroom</u>

241] Rivets for commonly used for structural work.

A] Countersunk head

B] Flat head

C] Pan head

D] <u>Snap head</u>

242] The caliper meant for measuring the width of a slot is...

A] Odd leg caliper

B] Outside caliper

C] Jenny caliper

D] <u>Inside calliper</u>

Calliper

243] The size of the dividers are specified by the -------

A] Total length of legs

B] Distance between the points when fully opened

C] Length of legs without points

D] <u>distance between the pivot and the point</u>

244] The instrument used to mark parallel lines, parallel to the datum edge is -

A] <u>jenny caliper</u>

B] Divider

C] Outside calliper

D] Inside calliper

245] Which one of the following is an indirect measuring tool?

A] <u>Outside caliper</u>
B] Vernier calliper
C] Steel rule
D] Outside micrometer
246] For cutting thin tubing, the most suitable pitch of the hacksaw blade is...
A] 1.8mm
B] 1.4mm
C] 1mm
D] <u>0.8mm</u>
247] For cutting solid brass, the most suitable pitch of the hacksaw blade is...
A] <u>1.8mm</u>
B] 1.4mm
C] 1mm
D] 0.8mm
248] A new hacksaw blade after a few strokes becomes loose because of the...
A] <u>Stretching of the blade</u>
B] Wing-nut threads being worn out
C] Wrong pitch of the blade
D] Improper selection of the set of saws.

Hacksaw frame

249] While cutting small diameter pipes, it is advisable to watch regularly and ensure that...
A] The cut is along the curved line
B] <u>More saw teeth are in contract</u>
C] The work is not overheated
D] Proper balancing of hacksaw is maintained

250] The vice clamps are used to...
A] Protect hard jaws
B] Clamp the work pieces rigidly
C] <u>Protect the finished surfaces</u>
D] Prevent the movable jaw being filed
251] The reference surface during marking is provided by the...
A] Surface gauge
B] Workpiece
C] Drawing of the work
D] <u>Marking table surface</u>
252] The size of an engineer's vice is specified by the...
A] Length of the movable jaw
B] <u>Width of the jaws</u>
C] Height of the vice
D] Maximum opening of the jaws
253] The part of the universal surface gauge which helps to draw a parallel line along a datum edge is the..
A] Rocker arm
B] Snug
C] Fine adjustment screw
D] <u>Guide pins</u>

Universal surface guage

254] Scribers are made of...
A] Mild steel
B] <u>High carbon steel</u>
C] Brass

D] Cast iron

255] Portion of the hammer used for fixing the handle is...

A] Face

B] Peen

C] Cheek

D] <u>Eye hole</u>

Hammer

256] Weight of the hammer for the marking purpose is...

A] <u>250g</u>

B] 500g

C] 1 kg

D] 2 kgs

257] The size of the dividers are specified by the...

A] Total length of the legs

B] Distance between the points when fully opened

C] Length of legs without the points

D] <u>Distance between the pivot and the point</u>

258] The included angle of the groove of 'V' block is always....

A] 45°

B] 60°

C] 90°

D] <u>120°</u>

259] 'V' blocks are available in grades of...

A] <u>A & B</u>

B] A,B & C

C] 1,2 & 3

D] 1 & 2

260] 'V' blocks of grade 'B' are made of

A] <u>Cast iron</u>

B] Mild steel

C] Steel

D] Cast steel

261] Name the punch used to locate the centre.

A] Prick punch 30°

B] Prick punch 60°

C] Centre punch

D] Dot punch

262] The point angle of centre punch is --------

A] 30°

B] 50°

c] 900

D] 1200

Centre punch

263] Punches are used for forming ---------of any shape

A] Holes

B] Mining

C] Knurling

D] Reaming

264] Generally the length of the handle of the vice is ----------

A] 1.5 times the normal size of the vice

B] 2.5 times the normal size of the vice

C] 3.5 times the normal size of the vice

D] 4.5 times the normal size of the vice

265] Bench vice spindle is made of ....

A] mild steel

B] Cast iron

C] Tool steel

D] Bronze

Bench vice

266] The convexity of files helps...
A] To file concave surfaces
B] To file convex surfaces
C] <u>To prevent rounding of edges of work</u>
D] The file to become straight when pressure is applied
267] Which file used for filling wood, leather and other soft material? .
A] Single cut file
B] Double cut file
c] <u>Rasp cut file</u>
D] Curved cut file
268] File used is used for ------------
A] Cleaning the work piece
C] Renewing the file teeth
B] <u>cleaning the file teeth</u>
D] Cleaning the chips

Files

269] File card is used to --------
A] Clean the work piece
C] Renew the file teeth

B] Clean the file teeth

270] The point angle of scriber is -----------

A] 30°

B] 60°

C] 5° to 10°

D] 12° to 15°

271] The cutting angle for chipping cast iron is...

A] 37.5°

B] 55°

C] 60°

D] 90°

272] The chisel will dig into the material when...

A] The rake angle is more

B] The clearance angle is too low

C] The angle of inclination is more

D] The angle of inclination is too low

273] A slight convexity is given to the cutting edge to...

A] Cut curved surfaces

B] Cut sharp corners

C] Prevent digging of the ends

D] Allow the lubricant to enter

274] Surface plates are made of...

A] High grade cast steel

B] Fine-grained cast iron

C] Alloy steels

D] Wrought iron

275] Surface plates are specified by their length and breadth & are in

A] decimetre

B] Cubic meter

C] Cylindrical

276] Ribs are given on the unmachined portion of the angle plate for...

A] Easy handling

B] Convenience in manufacturing

C] Clamping while setting on machines

D] Rigidity and to prevent distortion

277] The slots on the angle plate are given for...

A] Reducing weight

B] Aligning the work

C] Lifting using hooks
D] <u>Accommodating bolts</u>.
278] The size of the angle plates is stated by...
A] Weight
B] Length
C] Length x width
D] <u>Size number</u>
279] How many types of Lathe as per manufacturing?
A] Two
B] Three
C] <u>Four</u>
D] Five

<u>Lathe Machine</u>

280] How many types of Centre Lathe?
A] Two
B] Three
C] Four
D] <u>Five</u>
281] How many types of production lathe?
A] <u>Two</u>
B] Three
C] Four
D] Five
282] Which type of lathe is Roller Lathe?
A] Bench Lathe
B] <u>Special Lathe</u>
C] Production Lathe
D] Centre Lathe

283] For mass-production which machine is used?
A] Centre Lathe
B] Production Lathe
C] Special Lathe
D] Engine Lathe
284] Which lathe is used for more accurate job?
A] Centre Lathe
B] Special Lathe
C] Production Lathe
D] Tool Room Lathe
285] The accuracy of Tool Room Lathe is..] to Compeer Centre Lathe]
(A) Less
(B] More
(C) Very Less
(D) Equal
286] In Locomotive Assemble Wheel with Axel is turning on ......Lathe
(A) Centre Lathe
(B] Tool Room Lathe
(C] Wheel Lathe
(D) Gap Bed Lathe
287] Which following accessories is use for odd an uneven job turning?
(A) Three Jaw Chuck
(B] Two Jaw Chuck
(C) Driving Plate
(D] Face Plate

Lathe three jaw chuck
288] An irregular shaped work piece is turned on a Lathe] Which one of the following work holding accessories is used?

A] Two Jaw chuck
B] Three Jaw chuck
C] Driving plate
D] Face plate
289] The pads of a steady rest are made of
A] carbon steel
B] lead
C] mild steel
D] brass
290] A steady rest is used
A] to hold jobs
B] for face plate work
C] to drive the job
D] to support the job
291] A follower steady is held on the
A] lathe bed
B] lathe carriage
C] lathe spindle
D] tailstock
292] When turning long work pieces, the following is used
A sleeve
B change gear
C steady rest
D bracket]
293] The taper shank drills are held on the machine by means of...
A] Chucks
B] Sleeves
C] Drift
D] Vice
294] Drill chucks are fitted on the drilling machine spindle by means of
a...
A] Knurled ring
B] Arbor
C] Drift
D] Pinion and key

Drilling

295] The Morse taper provided on drills ranges between...

A] <u>MT 1 to MT 5</u>

B] MT 1 to MT 4

C] MT 0 to MT 5

D] MT 0 to MT 4

296] A drift is used for...

A] Drawing a drill location

B] Fixing chuck on the machine spindle

C] Removing a broken drill from the work

D] <u>Removing the drill from the machine spindle</u>

297] When the taper shank of the drill is larger than the machine spindle, the device to hold the drill is a...

A] Drill sleeve

B] <u>Taper socket</u>

C] Drill drift

D] Chuck and key

298] Accuracy or least count of a metric outside micrometer is ---------

A] 0-1 mm

B] <u>0.01 mm</u>

C] 0.001 mm

D] 0.02 mm

Micrometer

299] 1000 microns means -----

A] 1 mm

B] 1 m

C] 1000 mm

D] 10 cm

300] in a metric micrometer, a complete revolution of thimble advances -----------

A] 0.01 mm

B] 0.25 mm

C] 0.50 mm

D] 100mm

301] Ratchet Stop in the micrometer helps to ------------

A] Control the pressure

B] lock the spindle

C] Adjust the zero error

D] Hold the work piece

302] 1000 micron means ------------

A] 1 mm

B] 1 m

C] 1000 mm

D] 10 cm

303] What is the zero reading of a 50-75 mm outside micrometer?

A] 0000 mm

B] 001 mm

C] 2500 mm

D] 5000 mm

304] The value of the smallest division on sleeve of a metric outside micrometer is -----

A] 050 mm

B] 100 mm

C] 150 mm

D] 200 mm

305] Ratchet stop in the micrometer helps to ---------

A] control the pressure

B] Lock the spindle

C] Adjust the zero error

D] Hold the work piece

306] The graduations of a depth micrometer are...

A] Similar to an outside micrometer

B] In the reverse direction to that of the outside micrometer, both Thimble and sleeve

C] In the reverse direction only on the sleeve

D] In the direction only on the thimble

Depth micrometer

307] The least count of vernier calliper is (main scale = 49 division, vernier scale = 50 division]

A] 0.1 mm

B] 0.01 mm

C] 0.001 mm

D] 0.02 mm

Vernier Calliper

308] The type of measurement made by using a Vernier Calliper is -------
A] Direct measurement
B] Indirect measurement
C] 90"] (a] 81 (b]
D] None of these

309] The dial test indicator shows the measurement as
A] The actual size of the component
B] The difference between the two steps of 5 mm
C] The magnified small variations in sizes through a pointer
D] The direct reading of the dimension

Dial test indicator

310] V -block and dial indicator method is used to measure the
A] Length of the work piece ground
B] Circularity of the surface of the work piece
C] Flatness of the surface
D] Pitch of the thread

311] Which one of the following is not correct about dial test indicator?
A] It has 100 divisions on its dial
B] Motion of the stem is transferred to the dial through Gear train

C] Its accuracy is 01 mm

312] Which grade of slip gauge is generally used in workshop?

A] Grade 0

B] Grade l

C] Grade H

D] Grade 0

313] As per Indian Standards a special set gauge is used consisting of

A] 81 Pieces

B] 112 Pieces

C] 120 Pieces

D] 130 Pieces

Slip guage

314] The accuracy of reference gauge is

A] 005 mm

B] 001 mm

C] 0001]

D] 00001 mm

315] ln case of ant burr on slip gauge, it should be removed by

A] Filling

B] Lapping

C] Scraping

D] Grinding

316] Hardness of slip gauge should be?

A] More than 63 HRC

B] 58 HRC

C] 55 HRC

D] 50 HRC

317] ------------ Slip gauge is used for Checking component within an accuracy of 001 mm]

A] Workshop gauge

B] Inspection gauge

C] Reference gauge

D] Ring gauge

318] , ------------is used for checking accuracy of precision instrument]

A] Gauge block

B] Fader gauge

C] Sine bar

D] Plug gauge

319] Slip gauge are Cleaned before using to ensure accuracy] What medium will you use for this purpose

A] Oil

B] Thinner

C] Carbon tetrachloride/ White petrol

D] Turpentine oil

320] To check the dimensional accuracy of identical components, a dial test indicator is set-for t 6 Size and used as a comparator] What will you use to set to the dial test indicator?

A] Dial test indicator

B] Teeter gauge

C] Slip gauge

D] , surface gauge

321] which one of the following statement about Sine bar is not correct?

A] Uses tow precision rollers kept on either side

B] Made of the Chromium steel

C] The surface is lapped

D] The centrelines of the holes will be inclined to the top surface

Sine bar

322] A slip gauge is a ----------

A] Rectangular block

B] Square block

C] Cubic block

323] In 4th SERIES of slip gauge, which one of the following range is correct in set 46 pieces

A] 10 to 90 mm

B] 1001 101009 mm

C] 101 to 109 mm

D] '11'to_-19mm

324] In 5th SERIES of slip gauge, which one Of the following range is correct in set 46 pieces –

A] 100to 100 mm '

B] 1001 to 1009 mm

C] 101 to 009mrn

D] 11 to 9mm

325] In 2NDS SERIES of slip gauge, which one of the following range IS correct in set of 45 pieces-

A] 10 to 90 mm

B] 1001 to 1] 009 mm

C] 101 to 109 mm

D] 11 to 19mm

326] In 3RD SERIES of slip gauge, which one of the following range is correct in set 46 pieces –

A] 100 to 100 mm

B] 1001 to 1009 mm

C] 101 to 109 mm

D] 11 to 19 mm

327] In 1ST SERIES of slip gauge, which one of the following range is correct in set 46 pieces –

A] 0001mm

B] 001mm

C] 01mm

D] 10mm

328] In 2ned SERIES of slip gauge, which one of the following STEP is correct in set of 46 pieces –

A] 0001mm

B] 001 mm

C] 01 mm

D] 1-0 mm

329] In 3rd SERIES of slip gauge, which one of the following STEP Is correct in set 46 pieces
A] 0001mm
B] 001mm
C] 01 mm
D] 10mm
330] Sine bar is made of
A] high carbon steel
B] high speed steel
C] nickel steel
D] stabilized chromium steel]
331] Sine bar is used for
A] levelling the job for drilling
B] finding the angle of taper job
C] measuring diameter of holes
D] checking profile of thread]
332] Length of sine bar is the distance between
A] one end to another end of sine bar
B] diagonal cross length of the sine bar
C] centre to centre between rollers
D] outside to outside between rollers]
333] The size of a sine bar is specified by it's
A] weight
B] measurement of width
C] length
D] maximum angle of setting]
334] The purpose of providing a stopper at one end of the sine bar is for
A] easy handling
B] preventing the job from slipping]
C] supporting the slip gauge
D] using as a reference while setting]
335] A sine bar is made with four or five equally'spaced holes on its body] The purpose of these holes is to
A] Handle the sine bar easily
B] Reduce the weight of sin bar
C] Prevent distortion of the top surface of sine bar
D] Give good appearance to the sine bar
336] A sine bar is used for

A] Measuring the diameter of holes '
B] Finding the angle of a taper job
C] Leveling the job for drilling
D] Chuckin'g the profile of a thread
337] For measuring angles using the sine bar the angle framed according to the ratio between the height of slip gauge and the
A] Height of sine bar
B] Number slip gauge
C] Length of sine bar
D] Width of sine bar
338] ----------is used for checking angle within an accuracy of 1]
A] Gauge
B] Sine bar
C] Temple
D] Telescopic gauge
339] Centre line of the contact rollers and datum surface if the sine bar are
A] Same line' '
B] Parallel
C] Inclined
D] Perpendicular
340] The sine bar is made of -
A] High carbon steel
B] Stabilized chromium steel '
C] High speed steel
D] Nicked steel
341] The least count of a vernier bevel protractor is
A] 1"
B] 5'
C] 1∘
D] 5∘

Vernier bevel protractor

342] The part of a vernier bevel protractor which is normally used as a reference base for measuring angles is the

A] Blade

B] <u>Stock</u>

C] Disc

C] Main scale

343] The part of a vernier bevel protector on which main scale divisions are marked is the

A] Stock

B] Dial

C] <u>Disc</u>

D] Adjustable blade

344] The part of a bevel protractor, which comes in contact with the inclined surface while measuring is the

A] <u>Blade</u>

B] Stock

C] Disc

D] Dial

345] The value of each division of the main scale of a vernier bevel protractor is

A] 5'

B] <u>1°</u>

C] 5°

D] 10°

346] The value of each division of the vernier scale of a bevel protractor is

A] 1°

B] 1◦5'

C] <u>1◦55'</u>

D] 5'

347] Spindle is perpendicular to the work table

A] Horizontal milling machine

B] <u>Vertical milling machine</u>

C] Universal milling machine]

D] Lathe machine

Vertical milling machine

348] The table can be swivelled in horizontal plane

A] Horizontal milling machine

B] Vertical milling machine

C] <u>Universal milling machine</u>]

D] Lathe machine

349] The spindle is horizontal to the work table

A] <u>Horizontal milling machine</u>

B] Vertical milling machine

C] Universal milling machine]

D] Lathe machine

350] Rigid, sturdy and accommodates heavy work

A] <u>Horizontal milling machine</u>

B] Vertical milling machine

C] Universal milling machine]

D] Lathe machine

351] Boring, keyway cutting, profile milling can be done on this machine

A] Horizontal milling machine

B] <u>Vertical milling machine</u>

C] Universal milling machine]
D] Lathe machine
352] Helical grooves and gears can be milled on this machine.
A] Horizontal milling machine
B] Vertical milling machine
C] Universal milling machine]
D] Lathe machine

<u>Gear</u>

353] Slide movement on the column
A] Longitudinal feed
B] Cross feed
C] Vertical feed
D] Circular feed]
354] Slide movements on the knee
A] Longitudinal feed
B] Cross feed
C] Vertical feed
D] Circular feed]
355] Rotary table
A] Longitudinal feed
B] Cross feed
C] Vertical feed
D] Circular feed]
356] Table traverse]
A] Longitudinal feed
B] Cross feed
C] Vertical feed
D] Circular feed
357] Spindle is perpendicular to the work table
A] Horizontal milling machine

B] <u>Vertical milling machine</u>
C] Universal milling machine]
D] Lathe machine

358] The table can be swivelled in horizontal plane
A] Horizontal milling machine
B] Vertical milling machine
C] <u>Universal milling machine</u>]
D] Lathe machine

359] The spindle is horizontal to the work table
A] <u>Horizontal milling machine</u>
B] Vertical milling machine
C] Universal milling machine]
D] Lathe machine

360] Rigid, sturdy and accommodates heavy work
A] <u>Horizontal milling machine</u>
B] Vertical milling machine
C] Universal milling machine]
D] Lathe machine

361] Boring, keyway cutting, profile milling can be done on this machine
A] Horizontal milling machine
B] <u>Vertical milling machine</u>
C] Universal milling machine]
D] Lathe machine

362] Helical grooves and gears can be milled on this machine.
A] Horizontal milling machine
B] Vertical milling machine
C] <u>Universal milling machine</u>]
D] Lathe machine

363] Slide movement on the column
A] Longitudinal feed
B] Cross feed
C] <u>Vertical feed</u>
D] Circular feed]

364] Slide movements on the knee
A] Longitudinal feed
B] <u>Cross feed</u>
C] Vertical feed
D] Circular feed]

365] Rotary table
A] Longitudinal feed
B] Cross feed
C] Vertical feed
D] <u>Circular feed</u>]
366] Table traverse]
A] <u>Longitudinal feed</u>
B] Cross feed
C] Vertical feed
D] Circular feed]
367] helps to tool to lifts up during return stroke
A] <u>clapper box of shaper</u>
B] rocker arm
C] pawl and ratchet
D] bull gear
368] pivoted at the bottom of the base
A] clapper box of shaper
B] <u>rocker arm</u>
C] pawl and ratchet
D] bull gear
369] meant for feed mechanism
A] clapper box of shaper
B] rocker arm
C] <u>pawl and ratchet</u>
D] bull gear
370] helps to tool to lifts up during return stroke
A] <u>clapper box of shaper</u>
B] rocker arm
C] pawl and ratchet
D] bull gear
371] driven by pinion
A] clapper box of shaper
B] rocker arm
C] pawl and ratchet
D] <u>bull gear</u>
372] it carries the saddle
B] rocker arm
C] pawl and ratchet

D] bull gear

E] <u>cross rail</u>

373] it is mounted on bull gear face

A] clapper box of shaper

B] <u>rocker arm</u>

C] pawl and ratchet

D] bull gear

374] it slips during return stroke.

A] clapper box of shaper

B] rocker arm

C] <u>pawl and ratchet</u>

D] bull gear

375] Can be swivelled while shaping angular surfaces

B] Clapper block

C] Tool post

D] Hinged pen

E] <u>Swivel base</u>

376] it is a device for holding the cutting tool and for setting the depth and position of a cut

A] Clapper box

B] Clapper block

C] <u>Tool post</u>

D] Hinged pen

377] During return stroke the clapper box is free to swivel about it.

A] Clapper box

B] Clapper block

C] Tool post

D] <u>Hinged pen</u>

378] Holds the tool or tool holder rigidly

A] Clapper box

B] Clapper block

C] <u>Tool post</u>

D] Hinged pen

379] Lifts during of return stroke

A] <u>Clapper box</u>

B] Clapper block

C] Tool post

D] Hinged pen

380] Which one is the operation that cannot be done on the slotting machine?

A] key way slotting

B] dovetail slotting

C] gear cutting

D] <u>thread cutting</u>

Thread

381] Which one of the feed cannot be given to a slotter table with accessories

A] longitudinal

B] rotary

C] <u>vertical</u>

D] cross

382] The size of a slotter is specified by its maximum

A] longitudinal travel of table

B] height between table and ram

C] crosswise travel of table

D] <u>length of stroke of ram</u>

383] To slot a convex surface, the cutting tool required is

A] square nose tool

B] <u>round nose tool</u>

C] keyway tool

D] cornering tool

384] The convex surface can be slotted by using

A] longitudinal feed

B] <u>rotary feed</u>

C] cross feed

D] vertical feed

385] The purpose of quick return mechanism in a slotting machine is to

A] reduce the cutting time

B] have faster return stroke

C] maintain standard cutting speed

D] <u>reduce idle time having faster idle stroke.</u>

386] The main feed shaft of a slotting machine is drive by

A] bevel gear mechanism

B] <u>pawl and ratchet wheel mechanism</u>

C] tumbler gear mechanism.

D] worm and worm gear mechanism.

387] Loaded with spring

A] Plain or box type tool holder

B] Extension tool holder

C] <u>Relieving type tool holder</u>

D] Rotating tool holder]

Springs in drawing

388] For general purpose work

A] <u>Plain or box type tool holder</u>

B] Extension tool holder

C] Relieving type tool holder

D] Rotating tool holder]

389] Permits indexing for 90° at 4 positions

A] Plain or box type tool holder

B] Extension tool holder

C] Relieving type tool holder

D] <u>Rotating tool holder</u>]

390] For slotting larger circles

A] Plain or box type tool holder

B] <u>Extension tool holder</u>
C] Relieving type tool holder
D] Rotating tool holder]
391] Moves away the tool in the return stroke]
A] Plain or box type tool holder
B] Extension tool holder
C] <u>Relieving type tool holder</u>
D] Rotating tool holder]
392] Shielded metal arc welding is classified under the process of...
A] electric resistance welding
B] special welding
C] <u>electric arc welding</u>
D] electro gas welding
393] How to specify the size of an electrode holder?
A] by its weight
B] by its shape
C] <u>by its current carrying capacity</u>
D] by the metal used for making it
394] A voltage source produces an IR drop of 40V across a 20 ohms resistance, 60V across a 30 ohms resistance and 180V across a 90 ohms resistance all in series] How much is the applied voltage?
A] 180 V
B] 240 V
C] 100 V
D] <u>280 V</u>
395] The initial function of a choke in a tube light circuit is to...
A] limit the starting current
B] <u>induce high voltage</u>
C] heat up the filament
D] limit the current after starting
396] The peak-to-peak voltage is 99V] how big is the effective value of the sine wave?
A] 70 V
B] 44.5V
C] 49.5 V
D] <u>35 V</u>
397] A moving coil voltmeter reads 10 V AC] How big is the effective voltage?

A] higher

B] lower

C] the same

D] 10% higher

398] A capacitor is connected across a 200 volt AC line, its minimum voltage rating should be...

A] 100 volts

B] 200 Volts

C] 300 volts

D] 400 volts

399] How much is the nominal output voltage of a carbon zinc cell?

A] 12V

B] 1.5V

C] 2.0V

D] 2.2V

400] Cells are connected in series to..

A] increase the output voltage

B] decreases the output voltage

C] decrease the internal resistance

D] increase the current capacity

401] An unknown DC voltage is to be measured, which measuring range will you select first?

A] 500V

B] 50V

C] 1.5 V

D] 0.5V

402] Heat developed in a conductor is proportional to the...

A] square of the power

B] square of the resistance

C] square of the current

D] square of the time

403] The second function of a choke in a tube light circuit is to...

A] limit the starting current

B] induce high voltage

C] heat up the filament

D] limit the current after starting

404] A moving iron ammeter reads 10 A] how big is the peak current of the oscillation?

A] 7.07 A
B] 1.1414A
C] 70.7 A
D] 14.1 A
405] Power companies are interested in improving the power factor to
A] reduce line current
B] increase motor efficiency
C] increase volt-amperes
D] decrease power
406] In a RL parallel circuit, the opposition to total current is called...
A] reactance
B] resistance
C] a vector sum
D] impedance
407] An unknown direct current of micro ampere rating is to be measured, which measuring range will you select first?
A] 20 micro amp
B] 15 micro amp
C] 150 micro amp
D] 500 micro amp
408] The earth conductor provides a path to ground for..
A] leakage current
B] over current
C] high voltage
D] circuit current
409] Which appliance works on heating effect of electric current?
A] incandescent lamp
B] bimetallic thermostat
C] H R C fuse
D] toaster
410] connect two terminals of solenoid]
A] Pinion
B] Over running clutch
C] Plunger disk
D] Clutch
411] When the horn button is pressed the current flows to horn through
A] Horn switch
B] Solenoid coil

C] Battery

D] Chassis]

412] Turns core to magnet

A] Solenoid Switch

B] Actuating wire (when heated]

C] Ballast Resistors

D] Actuating wire (when cooled]

413] A capacitor increases the power factor value of an AC motor load when it is connected...

A] in series with the motor

B] in series with the starter

C] in parallel with the motor

D] in series with the main winding

414] Synchronous motor when used for power factor improvement should be...

A] under excited

B] over excited

C] loaded

D] running at no load

415] If a winding makes electrical contact with the metal case of the mixer motor the winding is...

A] grounded

B] open circuited

C] short circuited

D] loose connected

416] If the end shafts of a rotor turns blue it is an indication of...

A] scoring

B] overheating

C] freezing

D] burring

417] In the BIS system of limits and fits, the grade of tolerance are represented by number Symbols and there are ---------i

A] 14 grades of tolerance

B] 16 grades of tolerance

C] 18 grades of tolerance '

D] 20 grades of tolerance

Limit fit tolerance

418] A Product is said to have the quality when

A] Its shape and dimensions are within the limit

B] It is fit for use

C] It appears to be very good

D] The choice of material is right

419] The maximum clearance required between hole '30 +0021, 0000 and shaft 30 -0110, 0143 is

A] 0110 mm '

B] 0131 mm

C] 0164 mm

D] 0143 mm

420] A dimension is stated as 25 1002 mm in a drawing What is the tolerance?

A] +002 mm'

B] +004 mm

C] -002 mm

D] 2500 mm

421] A pin is fitted in a hole The tolerance zone of the pin is entirely above that of hole The fit obtained will be?

A] Clearance fit

B] Transition fit

C] Interference fit

D] Running fit

422] Tolerance is given to the part size to
A] Production the part within the required permissible size error
B] Increase the production
C] Decrease the Production
D] Finish the components approximately
423] Which one of the following is the clearance fit under the whole basic system?
A] 20 H7/p6'
B] 2067/211
C] ZOG/gll
D] 20H/g11
424] The three classes of fits as per BIS system aré
A] Clearance fit, interference fit and transition fit
B] Medium fit, push fit and tight fit
C] Flat fit, round fit and square fit
D] 'Sliding fit ', loose fit and shrinkage fit
425] Which one of the following tolerance specifications has a maximum dimensionless than 20 mm?
A] 20 +02,-03
B] 20 3202
C] 20 -02, 03 e
D] m 20 +500, ~03
426] Difference between the maximum and minimum limit is --------------------
A] Single informant
B] Basic shaft
C] Clearance
D] Tolerance
427] A shaft 55 running freely in bush bearing the type of fit is ---------
A] Clearance fit
B] Driving plate
C] shrinkage fit
D] None of the above
428] This allows positive transmission of power at larger angles.
A] Slip type coupling
B] Plate coupling
C] Clamp coupling
D] Universal coupling

429] This disengages automatically when the. torque is higher than the friction generated by the spring and jaw.
A] <u>Slip type coupling</u>
B]] Plate coupling
C] Clamp coupling
D] Universal coupling

430] This can be used only when the shafts are in perfect alignment.
A] Slip type coupling
B] <u>Plate coupling</u>
C] Clamp coupling
D] Universal coupling

431] This does not permit any axial movement of the shafts.
A] Slip type coupling
B] Plate coupling
C] <u>Clamp coupling</u>
D] Universal coupling

432] This is used in automobile vehicles.
A] Slip type coupling
B] Plate coupling
C] Clamp coupling
D] <u>Universal coupling</u>

433] Accommodates wheel hub bearings.
A] Kingpin
B] Spring pad
C] <u>Stub axle shaft portion</u>
D] Track rod ball joints

434] Pushes with drawal plate
A] Clutch cover
B] <u>Release bearing</u>
C] Release fingers
D] Clutch plate

435] Takes thrust load
A] Crankshaft
B] Flywheels
C] Torque wrench
D] <u>Thrust bearing</u>

436] Distributor shaft is supported by
A] ball bearing

B] shell bearing

C] <u>bush bearing</u>

D] needle bearing

Computer:-

Q.1. Which of the following is the biggest unit of memory?

A] <u>(Gigabytes)</u>

B] (bytes)

C](Megabytes)

D] (Kilobytes)

Q.2. The primery purpose of software is to turn data into.

A] (Website)

B] <u>(Infromation)</u>

C] (Programs)

D](Objects)

Q.3. GUI Stands for

A] <u>(Graphical User Interface)</u>

B](Greater User Interface)

C] (Graphical Union Interface)

D] (Graphical User Intereat)

Q.4. Key board keys that have arrows on them are called -

A] (Function Keys)

B] <u>(Navigation Keys)</u>

C] (Typewriter Keys)

D] (Special purpose keys)

Q.5. ASSCII, EBCDIC and Unicode are examples of Application Software's

A](True)

B]<u>(False)</u>

Q.6. The easiest way to access any part of the screen in the windows operating system is using the.

A] (Key Board)

B](Rat)

C]<u>(Mouse)</u>

D] (Joystick)

Q.7. A software is also called as a

A] (Procedure)

B] (Data)

C] <u>(Programs)</u>

D](Information)

Q.8. Back programs make copies of the files to be used in case the original files are damaged or lost.

A] (True)

B] (False)

Q.9. Microprocessor is often called as CPU

A] (True)

B] (False)

Q.10. .... Utility identifies unnecessary files on the hard disk and erases them based on users command.

A] (Backup)

B] (File Compression)

C](Uninstall Programs)

D] (Disk Clean up)

Q.11. This type of software is designes to help you be more productive tasks, and is widely used in nearly every discilive and occupation.

A] (Communication Software)

B] (Utility Software)

C] (Basic Application Software)

D] (System Software)

Q.12. Minicomputers are also known as.

A] (Mid Range Computers)

B] (Personal Digital Computers)

C] (Mainframe Computers)

D] (Laptop Computers)

Q.13. Which of the following device is used to play fast games on a computers.

A] (Touch Sruface)

B] (Touch Screen)2

C] (Track Ball)

D] (Joystick)

Q.14. Which of the following would not be consodered as portable computer.

A] (Desktop Computer)

B] (Note book computer)

C] (Personal Digital Assistent)

D] (None of these)

Q.15. Headphone is a typical output device.

A](True)

B](False)

Q.16. Uninstall programs helps us to remove unwanted programs installed in the computer.

A](True)

B](False)

Q.17. The capacity of a storage device is usually measured in terms of bytes.

A] (True)

B] (False)

Q.18. Capacity of the storage device is usually measured in terms of meter.

A] (True)

B](False)

Q.19............. is a pointing device.

A](Mouse)

B](Printer)

C](Scanner)

D] (Keyboard)

Q.20. The keyboards keys that are labeled F1, F2 and so on are called ....

A] (Function Keys)

B] (Numeric Keys)

C] (Typewriter Keys)

D] (Special purpose keys)

268] In diesel cycle Combustion takes place at

A] Constant pressure

B] Constant volume' '

C] Constant temperature

D] Constant temperature and pressure.

269] Rudolf Diesel, developed a Cl.engine

A] 1876

B] 1880

C] 1892

D] 1930

Engine in vehicle

270] Perkins built 'P' series engines
A] 1876
B] 1880
C] 1892
D] <u>1930</u>
271] N.A OTTO developed a 4 stroke cycle engine
A] <u>1876</u>
B] 1880
C] 1892

D] 1930

272] Dugald Clerk developed a 2 stroke cycle engine

A] 1876

B] <u>1880</u>

C] 1892

D] 1930

273] All cylinders in a horizontal line

A] 'V' Engine

B] <u>Inline Engine</u>

C] Opposed Engine

D] Radial Engine

274] Cylinders positioned in 'V' shape

A] <u>'V' Engine</u>

B] Inline Engine

C] Opposed Engine

D] Radial Engine

275] Cylinders positioned radially

A] 'V' Engine

B] Inline Engine

C] Opposed Engine

D] <u>Radial Engine</u>

307]Engine develops less power due to

A]<u>defective ignition timing</u>

B]excessive rich mixture

C]defective lubrication system

D]too tight cylinder head

308] Creates pressure on fluid

A] Brake pedal

B] <u>Master cylinder piston</u>

C] Wheel cylinder piston

D] Distribution block

309] Pushes master cylinder piston through linkages.

A] <u>Brake pedal</u>

B] Master cylinder piston

C] Wheel cylinder piston

D] Distribution block

310] Actuates the piston

A] Piston

B] <u>Push Rod</u>
C] Primary cup
D] Check valve
311] Develops pressure on fluid
A] <u>Piston</u>
B] Push Rod
C] Primary cup
D] Check valve

Piston & rings in Engine

312] Displacement volume of piston
A] |.H.P.
B] <u>Swept volume</u>
C] Mechanical efficiency
D] Horse power
313] Starting point of piston's downward movement in the cylinder
A] <u>T.D.C.</u>
B] Cycle
C] B.D.C.
D] Ignition
314] Starting point of piston's upward movement in the cylinder
A] T.D.C.
B] Cycle
C] <u>B.D.C.</u>
D] Ignition
315] Prevents blow by

A] Piston

B] Piston pin

C] Connecting rod

D] <u>Piston rings</u>

316] Reciprocates in the cylinder

A] <u>Piston</u>

B] Piston pin

C] Connecting rod

D] Piston rings

317] Connects piston and connecting rod

A] Piston

B] <u>Piston pin</u>

C] Connecting rod

D] Piston rings

318] Oscillates in cylinder

A] Piston

B] Piston pin

C] <u>Connecting rod</u>

D] Piston rings

319]The top and bottom halves of connecting rod are bolted on

A] crankshaft man journal

B] <u>crankpin journal</u>

C] camshaft

D] piston pin boss

320] A hole is drilled between crankshaft main journal and crank pin for

A] balancing of crankshaft

B] reducing crankshaft weight

C] <u>lubricating connecting rod bearings</u>

D] reducing crankshaft vibrations

321] Converts reciprocating motion into rotary motion

A] <u>Crankshaft</u>

B] Flywheels

C] Torque wrench

D] Thrust bearing

322] Rotary movement to pull and push action

A] Wiper motor

B] <u>Cranking link</u>

C] **Pinion**

D] Wiper blade

323] Accommodates wheel hub bearings.

A] Kingpin

B] Spring pad

C] Stub axle shaft portion

D] Track rod ball joints

324] Pushes with drawal plate

A] Clutch cover

B] Release bearing

C] Release fingers

D] Clutch plate

325] **Takes thrust load**

A] Crankshaft

B] Flywheels

C] Torque wrench

D] Thrust bearing

326]Distributor shaft is supported by

A] ball bearing

B] shell bearing

C] bush bearing

D] needle bearing

327] Stores energy

A] Crankshaft

B] Flywheels

C] Torque wrench

D] Thrust bearing

328] engages with the flywheel ring

A] Pinion

B] Over running clutch

C] Plunger disk

D] Clutch

329] Flywheel magneto consists of

A] Temporary magnet

B] Bar magnet

C] Permanent magnet

D] Needle magnet.

330] in flywheel magneto, the ignition coil is

A] stationary

B] Moving

C] Rotating

D] Oscillating.

331] To rotate the permanent magnet

A] Switch

B] Secondary coils

C]<u>Flywheels</u>

D] Condensers

332] While reversing the vehicle the driver should control

A] <u>Clutch</u>

B] Forward gear

C] Accelerator

D] Hand brake.

333] The clutch plate assembly has a centre steel disc riveted with springs for

A] strength

B] flexibility

C] less noise

D] <u>absorbing shocks</u>

334] Dog clutches are used in

A] <u>gear boxes</u>

B] friction clutches

C] brakes

D] differentials

Dog clutches in vehicle

335] Synchromesh mechanisms is provided for

A] Increasing the speed of the vehicle

B] Reducing the speed of the vehicle

C] <u>Smooth gear engagement'</u>

D] None of the above.

336] Only spur gears are used

A] <u>Sliding mesh</u>

B] Synchromesh

C] Double declutching

D] Transfer case

437] Which is the latest version of AutoCAD software?

a) 2016

b) 2017

c) <u>2018</u>

d) 2019

438] Which key is used to obtain properties palette in AutoCAD?

a) <u>Control+1</u>

b) Control+2

c) Control+3

d) Control+4

439] AutoCAD was first released in the year:

a) 1858

b) 1966

c) 1898

d) <u>1982</u>

440] How many units are available in AutoCAD?

a) 4

b) <u>5</u>

c) 7

d) 6

441] Which mode allows the user to draw 90° straight lines :

a) Osnap

b) <u>Ortho</u>

c) Linear

d) Polar tracking

442] To obtain parallel lines, concentric circles and parallel curves; __________ is used.

a) Array

b) Fillet

c) Copy

d) <u>Offset</u>

443] The default grid spacing in both X and Y directions is:

a) <u>10</u>

b) 20

c) 5

d) 15

444] How many workspaces are available in AutoCAD?

a) 2

b) 4

c) <u>3</u>

d) 5

445] Scale command can be accessed easily by typing:

a) SL

b) S

c) SC

d) <u>C</u>

446] Which command is used to divide the object into segments having predefined length?

a) Divide

b) Chamfer

c) Trim

d) <u>Measure</u>

447] How many grip points does a circle have?

a) <u>5</u>

b) 4

c) 3

d) 2

448] When drawing in 2D, what axis do you NOT work with?

A] X

B] Y

C] <u>Z</u>

D] WCS

449] The primary difference between the Model tab and the Layout tab(s) is _____.

A] the Model tab is used for drawing in 3D and a Layout is used for drawing in 2D

B] <u>the Model tab is where you create the drawing and a Layout tab represents the sheet that you will plot or print on</u>

C] the color of the background

D] the Model tab displays the drawing you are copying from and the Layout tab is where you lay out the new drawing

450] Which of the following is NOT a property of an object

A] Line weight

B] <u>Measure</u>

C] Hyperlink

D] Elevation

451] Which command convert discrete objects in polyline

A] Union

B] Subtract

C] Join

D] Polyline

452] To print the entire project, you will choose to regulate what to plot

A] Display

B] Extends

C] <u>Limits</u>

D] Window

453] What is the usefulness of viewports

A] <u>Allows us to see the screen or on paper different views of the same project</u>

B] Give us the ability to see projects have become a newer version of AutoCAD from our

C] We can make a change in one part of the plan, without affecting the rest

D] None of the above

454] What is the difference between the Scale command from the command Zoom

A] Scale for single object, while the Zoom whole plan

B] No difference

C] H Scale can grow / shrink a shape up 10 times, while the Zoom has no limits

D] <u>H Scale changes the size of objects, while the Zoom changes the visibility of the project</u>

455] When to fix a block attribute

A] <u>Before you fix the block</u>

B] When I make the block

C] After fix the block

D] No matter the number

456] What you cannot create from the command Offset

A] <u>Vertical straight</u>

B] Concentric circles

C] Three parallel lines

D] Parallel arcs

457] By what symbol shows the snap point to the closest point

A] with circles and dots in the center

B] With two triangle

C] <u>With three orthogonal</u>

D] With Diamond

458] Which state grid is use to design perspective

A] Parametric

B] <u>Isometric</u>

C] Pro-optic

D] Rectangular

459] If I want to draw a line in the direction 07:30 (local time) will give an angle

A] -135 degrees

B] 270 degrees

C] -225 degrees

D] None of the above

460] When in absolute Cartesian coordinates have points A (10.8) and B (6.5), then to make a line from A -> B with relative polar coordinates will write

A] @ -5 <36.88

B] @ 4 <30

C] @ 5 <216,88

D] @ 3 <60

461] What is the minimum allowable number of layers in a drawing

A] 0

B] 5

C] 1

D] 2

462] Which of the following is not a keyboard shortcut of AutoCAD?

A] Ctrl + P

B] Alt + F4

C] Ctrl + F4

D] Alt + B

463] Why do we have 16,7 M colors in RGB

A] Because so one can distinguish man

B] since this is the limit of graphics cards

C] For each color we have 256 shades and colors combination third

D] Because we want compatibility between PC and Macintosh

464] What setting gradient allows us to fill an open area?

A] Gap

B] Tolerance

C] Transparency

D] Open

465] What are the various options from left to right and the opposite direction?

A] Choose a different category of objects

B] select objects according to their color

C] <u>Select objects according to their position</u>

D] No difference

466] Which is corresponded to zoom mouse wheel?

A] <u>Zoom in / zoom out</u>

B] pan & scan

C] extents / all

D] scale

467] What command allows us to select objects based on some status?

A] Properties

B] Qselect

C] Pselect

D] Attributes

468] How to make a random line with an angle of 40 degrees to the x axis

A] will write 0 <40

B] will write 2 <40

C] <u>will write 3<40</u>

D] will write 4 <40

469] Which of the following file extensions cannot open the AutoCAD

A] dwg

B] dxf

C] <u>dot</u>

D] dws

470] A surveyor with a headband to measure the dimensions of a site, he make measurements by

A] <u>No one method</u>

B] Related Cartesian coordinates

C] Absolute polar coordinates

D] None of the above

471] What is the command used for Plagiostomi angle?

A] <u>Chamfer</u>

B] Fillet

C] Offset

D] Mirror

472] When should I use the Block Editor

A] To write text block

B] To fix outer block

C] <u>To fix dynamic block</u>

D] To store it in another version of AutoCAD

473] If the scheme that stores will be opened in AutoCAD 2006 then you must save it in

A] <u>AutoCAD 2004 dwg</u>

B] AutoCAD 2006 dwg

C] AutoCAD 2007 dwg

D] None of the above

474] Print scale 1:50 means that

A] The draft is 50 times less expensive than the original

B] <u>A 3 cm corresponds to half a meter</u>

C] A measure corresponds to 50 cm

D] None of the above

475] What do the letters UCS

A] Uniform Calculator System

B] United CAD System

C] Universal CAD Settings

D] <u>Universal Coordinate System</u>

476] What is the difference of two regular 8-gonon, which is one inscribed and another circumscribed circle

A] No difference

B] different opening angles

C] <u>different side length</u>

D] different crowd sides

477] If during the CCW measurement result gives an angle 135 degrees, the same CW angle measured is

A] 225 degrees

B] -135 degrees

C] -225 degrees

D] <u>135 degrees</u>

478] What does associative hatch

A] <u>Monitors the changes in shape that fills</u>

B] Relates to the other hatch plan

C] Both of the above

D] None of the above

479] What is the difference between command Plot and Print
    A] plot command prints only big plans
    B] The plot command for CNC (CAM)
    C] <u>No difference</u>
    D] print command can print up to A3 size paper

480] If you change the scale list a project that I have started from 1:50 1:10 then
    A] You will have to start over
    B] You should not raise the objects already exist (scale) by 5
    C] You will not need to change anything in hitherto methodology
    D] <u>should be converted into new items that will add based on the new scale</u>

481] Which of the following is NOT a unit of length measurement?
    A] Yards
    B] Parsecs
    C] Microns
    D] <u>Grads</u>

482] What does the command Wblock
    A] Warp-speed block
    B] <u>Write block</u>
    C] Window block
    D] Wide-area block

483] Where should you pay attention when you are working with autocad commands?
    A] Drawing area
    B] Status bar
    C] Tool bars
    D] <u>Command window</u>

484] Polar coordinates are used mostly for drawing______
    A] Arc
    B] Ellipse
    C] <u>Angular lines</u>

D] None of the above

485] How many SNAP points does an object have?
A] 1
B] 4
C] 5
D] <u>Depend on object</u>

486] How many points do you need to define for the rectangle command?
A] One
B] <u>Two</u>
C] Three
D] Four

487] How many AutoCAD objects are in a rectangle?
A] <u>One</u>
B] Two
C] Three
D] Four

488] How will you deselect an object while you are selecting set of objects?
A] Ctrl+ click on the object to be removed
B] <u>Shift + Click on the object to be removed</u>
C] Alt + Click on the object to be removed
D] None of the above

489] How long will a line from 0,5 to 5,5 be __________
A] 10 units
B] <u>5 units</u>
C] 15 units
D] None of the above

490] Objects are rotated around the
A] Bottom of the object
B] <u>Base point</u>
C] Center of the object
D] Origin

491] The origin of a drawing is at
A] <u>0,0</u>
B] 1,0

C] 0,1

D] 1,1

492] How would you select set of objects in a drawing?

A] <u>By a crossing window drawn from right to left</u>

B] By a crossing window drawn left to right

C] Shift+ clicking on the objects

D] None of the above

493] Fillet command can be used to obtain___________

A] Sharp corners

B] Round corners

C] <u>Both of the above</u>

D] None of the above

494] A polar array creates new objects_____

A] In a grid pattern

B] <u>In a circular pattern</u>

C] In a straight line

D] All of the above

495] How many layers a drawing should have?

A] 1

B] 2

C] <u>As many as depending on the complexity</u>

D] None of the above

496] Scaling objects make them_______

A] Smaller

B] Bigger

C] <u>Either smaller or bigger</u>

D] None of the above

INDUSTRIAL TRAINING INSTITUTE

Monthly Test-1, Marks- 20, Date:- _______________

(Every Question Carry Two Marks)

1-06] Benefit of SS system is ------

A] Increase in productivity

B] Increase in quality

C] Reduction in wastage of time

D] All of these

2-07] Safety is -----------

A] nobody's business

B] every bodise business

C] Some bodies business

D] The organization business

3-08] For basic categories of safety signs are available The meaning of"prohibition" sign ----

A] shows it must not be done

B] Shows what must be done

C] Warns the hazard or danger

D] Gives information of safety provision

4-09] Which one is a workshop safety?

A] Keep shop floor clean and free from grease, oil or other slippery materials

B] Stop the machine before changing the speed

C] Don't use cracked or chipped tools

D] Don't try to stop a running machine with hand

5-10] In Personal Protect Equipment (PPE] HELMET is used to

A] protect head

B] Protect eyes

C] Protect hands

D] Protect ears

6-11] Which of the following belongs to general safety?

A Have a worker in good attitude

B] The work clean and clear

C] Concentrate on your work

D] Keep the floor and gangways clean and clear

7-12] While grinding, which is used to protect the eyes?

A] Dark green glass

B] Mask

C] Sun glasses

D] Safety goggles

8-13] Which of the following is done for machine safety?

A] Check the oil level before starting the machine

B] Do things in a methodical way

C] Keep the floor and gangways clean and clear

D] Don't use dies and scarves

9-14] ln Personal Protect Equipment (PPE] , 'sleeves' is used to protect ----------

A] Face

B] Eyes

C] Ears

D] Hands

10-15] ABC stands for --------------

A] Automatic Breathing Control

B] Automatic Blood Control

C] Airway Breathing Circulation

D] Automatic Blood Circulation

INDUSTRIAL TRAINING INSTITUTE

Monthly Test-2, Marks- 20, Date:- _______________

(Every Question Carry Two Marks)

1-21] The grade of pencil is used to sketching lettering ....

a] conical point

b] chisel point

c] soft

d] low

2-22] For drawing thin lines of uniform thickness the pencil should be sharpened in the form of ....

a] chisel edge

b]conical

c] pointed

d] none of these

3-23] What is used for drawing curves which can not drawn by compass

a] small compass

b] French curve

c] protractor

d] none of these

4-24]Unnecessary lines is removed by .....

a] Duster

b] sand paper block

c] eraser

d] none of these

5-25] Circle and arcs are drawn by means of .....l.

a] compass

b] divider

c] lengthening bar

d]none of these

6-26] Inking pen is used in drawing ......

a] horizontal line

b] non circular arcs

c] vertical lines

d] all of these

7-27] The card board scale are available in set of .....

a] 7

b] 8

c] 6

d] 9

8-28] The convenient length size of 30 -60°-90° set square for used in school and colleges are......

a] 250

b] 200

c] 300

d] none of these

9-29] Drawing board is shape of ....

a] square

b] rectangular

c] triangular

d] none of these

10-30] The 'T' square , set square ,scale protractor are complain use in.......

a] protractor

b] mini drafter

c] set square

d] none of these

INDUSTRIAL TRAINING INSTITUTE

Monthly Test-3, Marks- 20, Date:- _______________

(Every Question Carry Two Marks)

1-36] When two sides of the hexagon are required to be horizontal the starting point for stepping equal division should be on an end of the.....

a] Horizontal diameter

b] Vertical diameter

c] Inclined diameter

d] None of these

2-37] If two sides of hexagon are required to be vertical the starting point should be on an end of the....

a] Inclined diameter

b] Horizontal diameter

c] Vertical diameter

d] None of these

3-38] The section obtained by the inter section of the right circular cone by a plane in different position relative to the axis of the cone are called.......

a] Conics

b] Circles

c] Triangles

d] Half circle

4-39] When the section plane is inclined to the axis and cuts all the generators on one side on a apex the section is in......

a] Conic section

b] Ellipse

c] Parabola

d] Hyperbola

5-40] When the section plane is inclined to the axis and is parallel to one of the generators the section is a ....

a] Ellipse

b] Parabola

c] Hyperbola

d] Cycloid

6-41] Use of elliptical curve is........

a] Arches

b] Dams and monuments

c] Manholes, gland & stuffing boxes

d] All of these

7-42] Use of parabolic curve is.........

a] Bridges & arches

b] Sound reflectors

c] Light reflectors

d] All of these

8-43] Use of hyperbolical curve is......

a] Cooling towers and water channel

b] Dames

c] Bridges

d] All of these

9-44] When the point is within the circle, the curve is called an.......

a] Superior trochoid

b] Interior trochoid

c] Trochoid

d] Isotrochoid

10-45] When the point outside the circle then the curve is called as......

a] Interior trochoid

b] Superior trochoid

c] Trochoid

d] Insuperior trochoid

INDUSTRIAL TRAINING INSTITUTE

Monthly Test-4, Marks- 20, Date:- ________________

(Every Question Carry Two Marks)

1-51] Eccentricity =

a] Distance of a point from the focus / distance of the point from directrix

b] Distance of focus from point / distance of point from

c] Distance of point from focus / distance of directrix of point

d] Distance of point from directrix / distance of point from focus

2-52] Mathematically an ellipse can be described by equation.....

a] $a2 / X2 + y2 / b2 = 1$

b] $x2 / a2 + y2 / b2$

c] $x2 / a2 + y2 / b2 = 0$

d] $x2 / a2 + y2 / b2 = 1$

3-53] Mathematically a parabola can be described by an equation......

a] $y2 = 4ax$

b] $x2 = 2ay$

c] $x2 = 4ay$

d] Both a & b

4-54] Mathematically hyperbola can be described by an equation.......

a] $x2 /a2 - y2 /b2 = 1$

b] $x2 /y2 - y2 /x2 = 0$

c] Both a & b

d] None of these

5-55] Cycloid can be described by an equation......

a] $y = a(1-cos Ø]$

b] $x = a(Ø -sin Ø]$

c] Both a & b

d] None of these

6-56] The mathematically represented hypocycloid is.....

a] $Y = a cos3 Ø, X = a sin3 Ø$

b] X = a sin3 Ø, Y = a cos3 Ø

c] X = a cos3 Ø, Y = a sin3 Ø

d] None of these

7-57] Mathematically represented by involute is

a] X = r sin Ø - r Ø cos Ø, Y = r cos + r Ø sin Ø

b] X = r sin Ø + r cos Ø, Y = r cos Ø – r Ø sin Ø

c] Y = r Ø cos Ø – r sin Ø, X = r sin Ø – r Ø cos Ø

d] X = r cos Ø + r Ø sin Ø, Y =r sin Ø - r Ø cos Ø

8-58] The lines from the object to the plane are called.......

a] Projection

b] Projector

c] Reference plane

d] None of these

9-59] The orthographic projection an object is represented by View on the mutual perpendicular projection lines

a] Two or three

b] Three or two

c] Three or four

d] None of these

10-60] When the projectors are parallel to each other & also perpendicular to the plane, the projection is called......

a] Isometric projection

b] Oblique projection

c] Orthographic projection

d] Perspective projection

INDUSTRIAL TRAINING INSTITUTE

Monthly Test-5, Marks- 20, Date:- _______________

(Every Question Carry Two Marks)

1-66] .... Method of projection is used in U.S.A & also in other countries.

a] plane of projection

b] Orthographic projection

c] First-angle projection

d] Third angle projection

2-67] When an object is situated on the ground, in first angle projection method, the bottom of its ..... will co-inside with XY

a] Top view

b] Front view

c] side view

d] All of these

3-68] The important element of this projection system

a] An object

b] Plane of projection

c] An observer

d] All of these

4-69] When line AB is parallel to HP hence ....

a] It' front view to AB

b] It''s side view equal to AB

c] It's top view equal to AB

d] None of these

5-70] When a line is parallel to a plane; it's projection on plane is equal to it's ;

a] True length

b] True shape

c] True size

d] None of these

6-71] The point is parallel in which the line or line produced meet the point is plane is called it's ....

a] Line

b] ratio

c] Trace

d] none of these

7-72] .... is the shortest distance between two points.

a] a line

b] a point

c] a straight line

d] none of these

8-73] When the line intersect horizontal plane that's called.....

a] horizontal trace

b] vertical trace

c] trace of line

d] none of these

9-74]Planes may be divided into two main types ......

a] Perpendicular planes, auxillary planes

b] Perpendicular plane, oblique planes

c] Auxillary planes , perpendicular planes

d] none of these

10-75] Planes which are inclined to the reference plane are called......

a] Auxillary plane

b] obliqeu plane

c] Perpendicular planes

d] picture plane

INDUSTRIAL TRAINING INSTITUTE

Monthly Test-6, Marks- 20, Date:- ________________

(Every Question Carry Two Marks)

1-81] The imaginary line of prism joining the centrs of the bases called.........

a] Faces

b] Axis

c] Apex

d] Base

2-82] A right & regular prism has it's axis....... to the bases

a] Parallel

b] Perpendicular

c] Inclined

d] None of these

3-83] When a pyramid or a cone is cut by a plane parallel to it's base thus removing the top portion, the remaining portion is called it's.........

a] Sphere

b] Cone

c] Cylinder

d] Frustum

4-84] Oblique cylinder & cones have their axes........ to their base

a] Inclined

b] Parallel

c] Perpendicular

d] All of these

5-85] Projection of two equal sphere s resting on the ground & in contact with each other, with the line joining there centre parallel to the..........

a] A VP

b] VP

c] HP

d] All of these

6-86] Projections of section on the other plane to which it is inclined is called.......

a] Section planes

b] Apparent section

c] True shape of sphere

d] None of these

7-87] When the section plane is parallel to the HP or the ground, the true shape of the section will be seen in.........

a] Front view

b] Side view

c] Top view

d] All of these

8-88] Surface of solid are laid out on a plane the figure obtained is called its........

a] Interpenetration

b] Development

c] Intersection

d] None of these

9-89] Development of surfaces is essential in.........

a] Foundry shop

b] Sheet metal work

c] Fitting shop

d] None of these

10-90] Which method of development used in transition pieces?

a] Parallel diameter

b] Radial line method

c] Triangulation method

d] Approximate method

INDUSTRIAL TRAINING INSTITUTE

Monthly Test-7, Marks- 20, Date:- ________________

(Every Question Carry Two Marks)

1-96] In engineering practice, objects constructed may have constituent part, the surfaces of which intersect one another in lines called........ of intersection.

a] Lines

b] Cones

c] Cylinder

d] Prisms

2-97] The line of interaction may be depending upon the nature of.......

a] Intersection surface

b] Intersecting solids

c] Intersection cones

d] None of these

3-98] The two plane surface intersect in a........ line

a] Curve

b] Straight

c] Plane

d] All of these

4-99] The line of intersection between two curved surface or between......... Surface and a curved surface is a curve.

a] A curved

b] A plane

c] A solids

d] None of these

5-100] When a solids completely penetration another solids there will be two lines of intersection. These lines are sometimes called the line or........

a] Line of interpenetration

b] Curve of interpenetration

c] Solids of interpenetration

d] All of these

6-101] Use of penetration curve is.......

a] Sheet metal work

b] Fitting shop

c] Fabricating work

d] Foundry shop

7-102] Methods of determining the line of intersection between surface of two interpenetration.........

a] Approximate method & radial line method

b] Line method and cutting plane method

c] Triangulation method and parallel line method

d] None of these

8-103] Example of interpenetration is..........

a] Two prism intersection

b] Cylinder and prism intersection

c] Cone and cylinders intersection

d] All of these

9-104] Two cylinder intersection is example of.........

a] Intersection

b] Interpenetration

c] Cone intersection

d] None of these

10-105] .... Method is explained in detail while solving illustrative problems

a] Line method

b] Radial line method

c] Cutting plane method

d] Parallel line method

INDUSTRIAL TRAINING INSTITUTE

Monthly Test-8, Marks- 20, Date:- _______________

(Every Question Carry Two Marks)

1-111] The major axis of the ellipse is long than...............

a] Radius of the circle

b] True diameter

c] Diameter of the circle

d] None of these

2-112] Makes practice for drawing of isometric view using........

a] Isometric planes

b] Isometric lines

c] Isometric graph

d] Isometric view

3-113] Use of parabolic curve is

a] Sound reflectors

b] Dams

c] Man hole of boiler

d] Gland & stuffing box

4-114] When the section plane is inclined the true shape of section on

a] AVP

b] VP

c] HP

d] A/P

5-115] When section plane is perpendicular to both the HP & VP the true shape of section on

a]Top view

b] Side view

c] Front view

d]None of this

6-116] When view projected on auxiliary planes are called

a] Auxiliary view

b Sectional view

c] Front view

d] None of these

7-117] Invisible features of an object are shown by means of

a] Outline

b] Chain lines

c] Hidden lines

d] None of these

8-118] Importance of sectional view on drawing for

a] Internal details

b] Outer details

c] Hatching

d] None of these

9- 119] The component is cut by a straight cutting plane is divided in to two parts

a] Half section

b] Full section

c] Offset section

d] Removed section

10-120] section line is two different parts (pieces] in contact should be drown in...

a] Same direction

b] Opposite direction

c]parallel direction

d] None of these

INDUSTRIAL TRAINING INSTITUTE

Monthly Test-9, Marks- 20, Date:- _______________

(Every Question Carry Two Marks)

1-126] The isometric projection is reduced in the ratio of

a] v2:v3

b] v3:v2

c] 1:v2

d] none of these

2-127] When measurements are required in three units the scale is used....

a] full scale

b] plain scale

c] half scale

d] none of these

3-128]Isometric drawing is larger in production about isometric projection is....

a] 22.5%

b] 0.815

c] 9/11

d] none of these

4-129] While isometric of sphere of spherical parts.......is must be used.

a] full scale

b] isometric length

c] true length

d] half scale

5-130] When circle draw with isometric scale the length of major axis of the ellipse to the ....

a] true diameter

b] isometric diameter

c] isometric diameter

d] none of these

6-131] In isometric view which contain a large number of non –isometric lines which method is used

a] box method

b] off-set method

c] co-ordinate method

d] centre lay out method

7-132] When drawing is drawn smaller than actual size of object .....

a] full scale

b] enlarging scale

c] reducing scale

d] none of these

8-133] When e=1 curve is called.....

a] parabola

b] hyperbola

c] ellipse

d] none of these

9-134]Compare with isometric drawing the advantage of oblique projection is....

a] front face is in true shape

b] two axis are always perpendicular to each othe

c] receding axis is taken at some convenient angles

d] none of these

10-135]If all the receding edges are drawn true length the oblique projection is called...

a] cavilier projection

b] cabinet projection

c] general projection

d] none of these

INDUSTRIAL TRAINING INSTITUTE

Monthly Test-10, Marks- 20, Date:- _______________

(Every Question Carry Two Marks)

1-141] In isometric view of hexagonal plane all the sides of hexagon is .....

a] equal length

b] unequal length

c] none of these

2-142] When all the faces are equal & regular the polyhedron is said....

a] regular

b] prisms

c] irregular

d] pyramid

3-143] Oblique prisms & pyramid have ......

a] axis perpendicular to the base

b] axis inclined to the base

c] faces inclined to the H.P

d] none of these

4-144] Icosahedrons has equal equilateral triangular faces

a] 12

b] 8

c] 20

d] 6

5-145] When a pyramid or cone is cut by a plane parallel to its base is called.....

a] pyramid

b] turned carted

c] frustum

d] none of these

6-146] Plane which are inclined to both the reference plane is called ......

a] oblique plane

b] perpendicular plane

c] inclined plane

d] none of these

7-147] When a line parallel to H.P & perpendicular to V.P the trace line is.....

a] V.T

b] H.T

c] no trace

d] V.T& H.T

8-148] When a line parallel to the V.P and inclined to H.P the true length of line in.....

a] front view

b] top view

c] side view

d] none of these

9-149] When point situated in front quadrant

a] above the H.P & in front of V.P

b] below the H.P & in front of V.P

c] behind the V.P & above H.P

d] below the H.P & behind the V.P

10-150] Find the quadrant of point "b" is 15 mm above H.P and 25mm behind the V.P

a] I st

b] III rd

c] IIII th

d] II nd

INDUSTRIAL TRAINING INSTITUTE

Monthly Test-11, Marks- 20, Date:- ________________

(Every Question Carry Two Marks)

1-Q.1. Which of the following is the biggest unit of memory?

A] (Gigabytes)

B] (bytes)

C](Megabytes)

D] (Kilobytes)

2-Q.2. The primery purpose of software is to turn data into.

A] (Website)

B] (Infromation)

C] (Programs)

D](Objects)

3-Q.3. GUI Stands for

A] (Graphical User Interface)

B](Greater User Interface)

C] (Graphical Union Interface)

D] (Graphical User Intereat)

4-Q.4. Key board keys that have arrows on them are called -

A] (Function Keys)

B] (Navigation Keys)

C] (Typewriter Keys)

D] (Special purpose keys)

5-Q.5. ASSCII, EBCDIC and Unicode are examples of Application Software's

A](True)

B](False)

6-Q.6. The easiest way to access any part of the screen in the windows operating system is using the.

A] (Key Board)

B](Rat)

C](Mouse)

D] (Joystick)

7-Q.7. A software is also called as a

A] (Procedure)

B] (Data)

C] (Programs)

D](Information)

8-Q.8. Back programs make copies of the files to be used in case the original files are damaged or lost.

A] (True)

B] (False)

9-Q.9. Microprocessor is often called as CPU

A] (True)

B] (False)

10-Q.10. .... Utility identifies unnecessary files on the hard disk and erases them based on users command.

A] (Backup)

B] (File Compression)

C](Uninstall Programs)

D] (Disk Clean up)

INDUSTRIAL TRAINING INSTITUTE

Monthly Test-12, Marks- 20, Date:- ________________

(Every Question Carry Two Marks)

1-486] How many points do you need to define for the rectangle command?

A] One

B] Two

C] Three

D] Four

2-487] How many AutoCAD objects are in a rectangle?

A] One

B] Two

C] Three

D] Four

3-488] How will you deselect an object while you are selecting set of objects?

A] Ctrl+ click on the object to be removed

B] Shift + Click on the object to be removed

C] Alt + Click on the object to be removed

D] None of the above

4-489] How long will a line from 0,5 to 5,5 be __________

A] 10 units

B] 5 units

C] 15 units

D] None of the above

5-490] Objects are rotated around the

A] Bottom of the object

B] Base point

C] Center of the object

D] Origin

6-491] The origin of a drawing is at

A] 0,0
B] 1,0
C] 0,1
D] 1,1
7-492] How would you select set of objects in a drawing?
A] By a crossing window drawn from right to left
B] By a crossing window drawn left to right
C] Shift+ clicking on the objects
D] None of the above
8-493] Fillet command can be used to obtain___________
A] Sharp corners
B] Round corners
C] Both of the above
D] None of the above
9-494] A polar array creates new objects_____
A] In a grid pattern
B] In a circular pattern
C] In a straight line
D] All of the above
10-495] How many layers a drawing should have?
A] 1
B] 2
C] As many as depending on the complexity
D] None of the above

www.ingramcontent.com/pod-product-compliance
Lightning Source LLC
Chambersburg PA
CBHW052028150726
48002CB00002B/505